# CLANG!

## SMILEY DROPS A FEW

By

STEVE 'SMILEY' BARNARD

This book is dedicated to

Alan Thompson and Danny Schultz

First published 2020
ISBN 978-1-9993046-2-1

Published by
GATECRASH THE PARTY BOOKS
www.gatecrashthepartybooks.com

# CLANG! Smiley Drops A Few

Foreword by Karl Parsons

It's always exciting being asked to write the foreword for a book, especially a Rock & Roll one. But it's a bit like being asked to be best man at a wedding. You get all fluffy, excited and emotional, then it suddenly dawns on you you've got to stand up and say something.

So here goes:

In the thirty odd years I have been working in and around the Music Industry it's impossible not to drop the odd name into a conversation. Yes, it's met with the occasional roll of the eyes skywards, but invariably the recipient of said information takes it on the chin graciously.

And come on, we've all done it haven't we?

Now I guess I am perfect for this introductory role. Not because I know the writer Steve 'Smiley' Barnard really well, and because he makes me laugh, but for the sole reason that I am his go to Album Cover designer. I invariably get to hear the juicy music interaction in detail, and the eclectic stories that go with it.

What you have to understand before you dive deep into these pages is Smiley is almost chameleon like. Working independently on multiple levels, with a myriad of different music influencers, that all share a common love for the boy, as I do!

Clang represents an open mic opportunity for a host of anecdotes, wit and charm that befits the working life of one of the UK's finest drummers. Who (if you've ever watched him perform live) commands solo attention. Yet if you are ever fortunate enough to meet him he offers humility and respect to his fellow man. A noble attribute in an industry not noted for such grace.

When Smiley first mentioned to me that he was going to write a book about all the 'musos' he's crossed paths with, I got all fluffy and excited again! Because like you, I cannot wait to get me teeth into these memoirs.

With that in mind I will leave it there.

SUNSHINE CORNER STUDIOS 2020

CHAPTERS

# CHAPTER 1
## ... THE SON OF A PREACHER MAN

I was only ever good at one thing. It was the only consistent from my early days as far back as I can recall. There was always a wooden spoon or stick shaped object in each hand hitting the nearest available surface in an early paradiddle style.

It took me till the age of 24 to realise that not only was I not gonna be a professional footballer or be the 13th man to walk on the moon. I had discovered I was rubbish at paper rounds, table waiting, shelf stacking, paper folding, menswear sales junioring, data prepping, hardware selling, concrete repairing, warehouse assisting, tele-salesing, office equipment selling, warehouse managing, lift repairing and auto factor delivering ... add into that equally as rubbish at stints in bar tending, washing up, computer inputing, and any other part time bob earner, and you'll get the picture that music was the only career for me.

Whilst masquerading in all these varying degrees of employment rubbishness, I was playing my drums. Whether it be after work in local scout huts with local bands, or after school in our loft converted house in Sunbury on Thames, living with my incredibly patient and understanding Mum and Dad, who always helped me pursue my true (and only) real calling in life whist putting up with me impersonating large fields of sprawling wildebeest roaming across the Serengeti 2 flights upstairs ... or drumming along to Big Country as I liked to call it. Home really was where the heart was.

We were a close family, with my sister and twin brothers thrown into a very loving pot of graciousness, love, and, intriguingly, a baptist upbringing. See, my Dad was the Reverend Mike Barnard. I was, and still am, an actual son of a preacher man (sounds cooler if you sing it). It had its tricky moments. You see my Dad was held in a messiah like status by many, and as a Church group leader in our youth, was surrounded by impressionable teenagers living of his every word.

Want an example? I was probably 17. The phone in our kitchen rings and I dutifully answer.

'Hello.'

'Oh, hi, it's Karen, is Mike there?'

'Hang on Karen. Dad, phone call for ya.'

'Who is it mate?'

'It's Karen.'

'Who?'

'Karen, from church.'

'What does she want?'

'I don't know.'

'Well ask her for me.'

'OK Dad. Hello Karen, he's a bit busy at the mo, what do you want?' (Always had a way with words me).

'Well,' said Karen, 'I'm in a shop, and I've got a blue dress and a red dress, and I wanted Mike to tell me which one the Lord thinks I should buy?'

'Hang on Karen. Dad, Karen is in a shop, she has a blue dress and a red dress, and she wants to know which one the Lord thinks she should buy?'

Small pause.

'THE BLUE ONE.'

Yep, that was what it could be like being the son of the messiah. I think the messiah's followers slowly worked out between the years of 1968 and 1986 that little Stevie (Smiley wasn't born by this point) wasn't quite in the same messiah-like league as his Dad, by quite a few leagues actually. The Son of God like status was fun while it lasted, but I was exposed by my lacking in being able to tell you what Matthew 3 v24 was really trying to say to us, and, by that point, girls.

Let's skip the school bit. I never really liked school, and school never really liked me. There weren't any other musicians in our school so, as I started getting more and more into the fashion and culture that music inspired in me, the more I stood out like a hungry bridesmaid at a free wedding buffet.

I got away with it until about fourteen, and then the puddings came out shall we say, because by that point I was hanging around with older boys, boys who had left school, boys who had girlfriends, and cars, and were super cool (in the eyes of the 14 year old son of the messiah); maybe not quite so much when I now look back at the old photos (check for yourself, I may be missing something that may have been strangely in vogue, but I doubt it).

It's by looking back at said photos for the research purposes for this book that I notice just how confused I was. No wonder all the casuals at school listening to Luther Vandross and Imagination didn't want me to go to the Walton Hop with them on a Friday night, because you see, I was what I've now christened, a 'newrogothic'. This is what you become when you are listening to cool bands like Echo and the Bunnymen, The Waterboys, The Alarm, Spear of Destiny, U2, The Jam and The Violent Femmes, whilst secretly liking the look of your sister's favourite New

Romantic bands, like Duran Duran and Spandau Ballet. So, if you confusingly merge those worlds of music and fashion you get 'newrogothic'. This basically involved sleeveless black T-shirts being coolly worn by Bono and Mac, with skinny black jeans and pointy black suede boots. Not too radical I hear you say. Bear with me; it gets a bit trickier. Add to this my new floppy fringe (those were the days...) being dipped into a bowl of fresh peroxide pretty much every day after school to get THAT John Taylor effect whilst pretending it was THAT Bono effect. Add to this (you so know where this is going) EYE LINER... or as it's now known GUY LINER. As I said this probably doesn't sound too radical to all you old punks and skins out there in your 50's with no fringe, or any hair for that matter, but at the time, in my confused newrogothic world, it was tricky, mostly due to the fact I was now working after school in the local supermarket, stacking shelves and generally being a bloody rebel. Yes, I was wearing guy liner whilst stacking, as was pointed out by a 6-year-old at a very loud 6-year-old level. It was like that scene in Quadrophenia when Jimmy is on the train, 5.15 by The Who blaring out as he is off his head on drugs and rebelling against the world; but in the supermarket, whilst stacking shelves. The most horrifying recollection of this event isn't being called out by a 6-year-old, it was that I had now switched from black guy liner to blue. I shit you not. Nick Rhodes pulled it off. I didn't, but then Nick was never renowned for his shelf stacking abilities.

My new compadres in Rock & Roll fashion were in a band, and the church youth club, but more importantly to the son of the messiah, a band, a proper band, like U2 and The Alarm, and nothing like Duran Duran. Original songs written by cool 19-year-old guys about which a 14-year-old shelf stacking newrogoth son of a preacher man had absolutely no scooby doo what they were about, but they were cool. They had a cool name, VOX HUMANA. Nope, didn't know what that meant either, but they wanted me to be the drummer. Was it my bleached fringe or eye liner? Or the fact no one else in the church group had ever attempted a double paradiddle let alone own a premier kit? I'll let you decide that one. So there we were; Marc with a C, Mark with a K, Trevor, and me.

Now the Vandross brigade back at Kenyngton Manor really didn't know how to take my new-found stardom, or give a flying f**k, until, we had a badge. Yes, a badge. Not a 12-inch vinyl or 3 foot poster, a badge. It was basically a black and white image of 3 cool, 6ft, 19-year-olds, a 5ft newrogoth, whose voice hadn't broken yet and an 8ft cross. Yeah. That's how Vox Humana rolled, and all the casuals (I say all as you weren't there and can't prove me wrong) suddenly thought I was cool. I WASN'T.

By the time I left Kenyngton Manor Vox Humana had been in the studio, my first studio experience. I can't remember if it was Abbey Road? It wasn't, it was a shed in some guys garden in Twickenham. We bashed a few tunes out. Trevor could probably tell you their names, and chord sequences, but I, sadly, don't recall, which leads me to believe they were never smash hits. We then did some gigs, in pubs. I wasn't old enough to buy a pint, let alone strut around like a brooding Rock Star, so I kind of hid behind Mark, with a K, and waited for puberty to kick in. It took its bloody time I can tell you.

By the time I was shopping for shaving foam I had had about 8 jobs and was in my 12th band. So I will pop Vox Humana in the 'where are they now' file for safe keeping, until they read this and put it all over Facebook that they are alive and well and still my close pals; well, the 2 of them who spell their names properly. I can hear my Mum's early 1986 words of wisdom, around the time of Live Aid. 'You know if you keep putting your fringe in peroxide your hair will fall out'. What do parents know eh?

Right, we need some 'clanging' to get this party started.

Everyone knows someone famous. When you're growing up your Mum and Dad always know someone who is a household name. Here we go. The first of many. CLANG! ... PAUL GODDARD. Yep. Paul Goddard. Obviously you all know who he is but, for the handful of you who don't, he played for QPR and my Dad worked with his brother Graham. Yep, it was like knowing Mick Jagger. We even went to his wedding (We didn't, we went and stood in the field over the road from the church with the other five hundred QPR fans).

That was our first taste of fame, but then in my early teens, CLANG! ... CHIP HAWKES. Yes, the singer with The Tremeloes. Mick Jagger my arse. This man was a bona fide legend. Rock Star house, Rock Star wife (or Auntie Carol as I knew her) and 3 Rock Star kids, one called Chesney (do the maths). So our Sunday afternoons were spent at the biggest house I had ever seen, swimming in their big Rock Star swimming pool. They were special, and now we were too, by association. Its ironic now because if I ever try to clang my kids with a celebrity name their Rock n

Roll Dad has met on his Rock n Roll travels, all I get is a shrugged shoulder or a 'who?'.

Apart from; CLANG! ... SIA. My youngest daughter, Lola, thought it was cool that I played drums for her once. I did, but I may have embellished the story slightly for my wide eyed 9-year-old, looking longingly into her cool-as-chips Dad's eyes.

My eldest daughter Georgia thought it was cool to have received a card from, CLANG! ... ROBBIE WILLIAMS, when she was born. That's probably the last time she thought I was cool, in 1999. Anyway, where were we? Let's pop ourselves into the most Rock n Roll of days.

LIVE AID. We can all recall where we were, what we were wearing and how blonde our fringe was now, right? I loved Live Aid. I watched it from start to finish. I sat dreaming of drumming for U2, then Bowie, then The Who; before taking Phil Collins' place on Concorde, travelling to America to play with Led Zeppelin (if you get a chance to read Phil Collins' book, it's well worth it for the story he tells about his Live Aid experience). There you go Phil, that might sell another couple of books for you. Happy to help.

Anyway, Live Aid was a magical day. As I recall, I didn't actually drum for anyone that day as I was, at that point in my Rock & Roll journey, working in the Menswear section of a department store whilst doing a typing course, with a bleached fringe. I was probably in a band but, if I was, I can't remember, and, if I can't remember, then I don't expect you to. I know I was on my journey of surfing rubbishly through rubbish jobs, unknowingly toward musical pastures yet untrodden. Even I'm impressed with that sentence.

So, let's skip on to around 1990'ish. I was working as a salesman, as I got a free car, but I hated that job more than any other. Think of the words 'Gareth' and 'Cheeseman' and anyone with a hint of cool affection for alternative comedy will understand. I was living with my mate Andi, with an I. He was the singer of Potato Joe. Yes, THAT Potato Joe. We were a great band, but Matt and Sandra had got married and our greatest fears started to raise their newly married head. Rehearsals were becoming a bit of an inconvenience to a newly married couple. It was then that I got my first SLIDING DOOR MOMENT.

A guy called Steve who knew of me but not I of him wanted me to audition for his band, Intimate Strangers. Now I say sliding door moment not particularly because of the million selling debut album by the Strangers, more to do with the new set of friends which came with the band and their regular weekend gigs. People who would ultimately stay in my life to this present day, friends who knew me as a reluctant salesman and as the drummer for that fella from Take That on Top of the Pops. The friends who thought it would be hilarious, at an Intimate Strangers gig in Feltham one evening, to set the drummer up by wheeling out a piano for the encore, and then ushering him on to play 'Let it be' in front of five hundred people. That's the sort of jolly jape my new friends used to pull on me regularly. Having said that, the Beatles moment turned into a strange moment in time, with a tenth of the audience joining me behind the piano for a Live Aid type sing along, some with tears and a whole lot of loving going on. I remember that moment vividly, like my first taste of a drug, knowing I wanted more. Since that evening the one thing that has kept the Cassells', Speight's, and Treasure's, and all the Ashford massive, close to me and my heart, is the fact that they have never stopped taking the piss. They started strongly and kept that level to an Olympic standard that remains, as does our friendships, as strong today as the first time Jain Cassells, the better half of Dave Cassells, or as we know him, Cass, called me a knobhead. Now that's what you call a true friend.

## CHAPTER 2
## ... SLIDING DOORS

So, I reckon its 1990, as I said before I have a shocking memory for dates, times and places; oh, and remembering to get milk when Kerry has only asked me 20 minutes ago. Just to get this straight at an early point in the book, Kerry is my wife. She also answers to the name Kezza, Kez and Kezzawoo. So now you know. Future confussion avoided.

I do however have a brilliant memory for sporting occasions, hence it's Italia 90. Gazza has just started crying, Lineker is looking at Bobby Robson and mouthing "have a word with him", and I am in the Speight lounge with 2 Speights and a Cassells. I remember this well because, when England scored, we all shot up from the sofa and punched the air, and dear old Ma Speight's glass light shattered into a million pieces. She was in the room like Usain Bolt and as we stood in a line with our arms behind our backs, she walked along the line, eyeballing us individually like the scary army fella in An Officer And A Gentleman. We all stood firm. Nobody flinched. Surrounded by shards of glass, with a lonely lightbulb gently swaying above our heads, she uttered the immortal line 'Show me your hands'. There was a silence. Then forty fingers were sheepishly revealed, one of which, belonging to Phil's left hand, was now the colour of a cheese and wine party at Oliver Reed's house. We all laughed. Ma Speight didn't. That was the last sporting event in the now dimly lit Speight lounge.

It being 1990 I was now well into my rubbish job list, this time warehouse supervisor (probably a self-proclaimed, totally made up, title for bloke in warehouse) at a Christian company called CWR. I bet you're thinking I had used my 'son of the messiah' status to pull on those Christian strings, but it was actually nothing to do with my legendary, seriously dwindling, baptist status. It was more about the fact that Potato Joe Matt was the boss, and he was feeling a bit guilty about the, newly-wed, lack of Potato Joe rehearsal scenario.

There were some lovely people at that firm, well three, and a whole bunch a crazy Christians who saw me as more son of Satan than Billy Graham's godson. They used to start the day with a prayer meeting. Now I'm all for that in anyone's world but they were kicking off at eight forty-five and I was generally slipping in the side door at about five past nine. Tricky things to sneak into, prayer meetings. Don't be fooled by all that eyes closed, hands in the air business. They all had at least one eye open and it was focused directly at me. There are only so many times you can pull the 'do you know who my Dad is?' card. Not sure how long I lasted.

The World Cup had finished and that was my way of remembering 1990. Then my little Sis announced she was moving to Australia for a year. 'Good on you Sis' I thought. Her announcement was soon to be followed by my redundancy, and with a bit of redundancy cash in my pocket, next stop, SYDNEY. I only went for a month, but it was ace. Soobie, my Sis, was travelling with a couple of stoners. SLIDING DOOR MOMENT ... one being the legendary Aussie Mick. Brother to Aussie Liz who was then singing with me in Intimate Strangers. You remember them yeah? So, the connection had been made and I bagged myself a new best friend. An Aussie. I believe everyone should have an Aussie best friend. They are the best. They look at life in a slightly more, well, Aussie way. Everything is a positive. Your beer glass is nearly empty? Ah mate that's great news, let's get another one in. Life advice Aussie style is brilliant. When dull Dave came round to ours for some relationship advice, the conversation was along these lines;

'and so that's why I am so heartbroken, Lydia and I have come to an end.' (That story went on for about 2 hours and 15 beers). 'What should I do? Mick, any advice as you haven't said a word for a hundred and eighty minutes?'

'Yeah, get over her, go out with someone else!'

Claire Raynor eat your heart out. I'd travelled half the world to see my Sis but had actually spent most of the time with my new bezzie. They are so friendly, Australians. Mick always knew how to get a free beer.

'G'day guys this is Steve, he's a Pom.'

Laughter and piss taking out of the way and there were instantly two Tooheys Red Stripe's on the table. I learnt a lot from that boy. Still do to this day. I don't necessarily ask his advice for obvious reasons, but a better friend you couldn't ask for. Unless his name was Simon and he played drums.

I had moved back to the UK, my friendship with my little Sis still intact (just) and had moved onto driving a van, delivering car parts. Musically, it was a bit of a dull time. I was playing for a few bands who I, and certainly you, would not recall; but then, through a tenuous studio connection, I got a call from Paul King. Paul was a former member of 'In The summertime' 70's folk legends Mungo Jerry. He had a little pub band called The Skeleton Crew who were looking for a drummer to sit in the coming Friday. This sounded interesting. He said they were playing the night before in Ascot if I fancied checking them out. So off I went to the racing mecca of Berkshire to embrace my next SLIDING DOOR MOMENT. The drummer had a huge white kit, it was so much better than mine. He was handsome and suave. I had moved on from all things 'newrogothic' by now but wasn't what you would say yet 'on it', fashion wise. What fascinated me most about the kit wasn't the 20" kick drum, or the five Tama toms ranging from 8" to 16". No, it was the ashtray clamped just below the splash cymbal allowing our drummer to get through half a pack of silk cut lights by the interval. I decided to have a wee. I walked in the gents and there he was. The smoking drummer. Resplendant with Zildjian jacket and still wearing his drumming gloves. Silk cut in mouth he turned towards me, popped the boys back in the barracks and without a whiff of imperial leather entering the scenario he boomed 'Hi. I'm Simon'. A new bezzie right there and then.

We sat down and ordered a couple of large cokes. I was driving, he was drumming, and we began to chat. Simon was extremely well spoken and well educated. He had owned a wine bar, drove a Saab, and lived in a flat overlooking the River Thames. What a guy. Then the question that turned my future on its head.

'So Si,' (we were already at the name shortening point) 'do you do many of these kinds of gigs?'

'Sure,' he replied, 'pretty much six nights a week, in about ten or eleven bands.'

The planet paused in its spin cycle as I comprehended his statement; 'and you get paid for all these gigs?'

'Well the Saab doesn't run on Coca cola does it?' he may have said. He probably didn't but it made me laugh, and Si when he reads this. As the planet re-established its spin cycle my brain didn't. Si had climbed behind his ashtray drums and was smashing his way through ten more silk cuts with what was to become my new band the following day. You see, Si was about to go to university to become a teacher, and I was about to take ten or eleven bands off his nicotine stained hands. The future was bright... The future was Pub Rock and, boy, did I embrace it.

Every band opened a whole new world of friends. Every gig was a wide-eyed opportunity to play, and get paid, in front of new faces who, thanks to Facebook, I can distantly remember to this day. And so, after being swiftly relieved of my driving duties at Camberley Auto Factors for inadvertently asking Derek the sweaty boss if he wanted me to pick up some deodorant on my next excursion to some grubby country garage, I was now officially A MUSICIAN. My job title; MUSICIAN. Earning capability; MUSICIAN. Wink and cheeky smile to the lady in the paper shop every morning.

'Yeah, I look tired cos I was out late gigging, cos I'M A MUSICIAN.'

There I was, drummer with ten or eleven badly named bands, made up, mostly, of MUSICIANS signing on, as well as sons of famous people, and sons of publicans.

'You can play our pub, but my Davey has to play bass.'

Fair enough. 'Do you know Freebird Davey? It's in G'.

The main two bands at this point couldn't have been further away from each other in social standings. In the Blue corner I give you SPINOUT. The band comprising of, CLANG! ... ZAK STARKEY, ... son of RINGO STARR; ... GARY ROBERTS ... son of RUSS ABBOTT; and ... GARY NUTTALL ... future ROBBIE WILLIAMS guitarist. The blue corner was a brave new world for the newly named SMILEY.

Let's get this out of the way. The rename is alleged to have been acted out like this; maybe use Peter Ustinov and Gregory Peck in the lead roles. Clears throat, and action. The setting, The Blue Anchor pub in Staines. The year, probably 1991'ish. I'll check who was in the Cup Final. Here we go.

Ustinov: 'You know that drummer Steve?'

Peck: 'Which Steve?'

Ustinov: 'Drummer Steve, Smiley Steve.'

Quick shorten over the next month or two and he was born. SMILEY. Not quite the showbiz naming ceremony we were all hoping for I know but, nevertheless, he is now amongst us. And, of course I played up to this newly given moniker. I crafted that cheeky grin to perfection. It would be used later in life whilst miming badly on television. It was honed.

Anyway, back to the Blue corner. Spinout were cool. I used to go around to Zak's house all the time. I remember pulling up outside one afternoon as he was waving away a blacked-out Mercedes. 'You just missed my Dad' he said, as casually as he may have said 'I see we lost a wicket in the cricket'. I had been that close to a bona fide, living, breathing, Beatle; and that, my friends, is definitely worthy of a CLANG!

Now over to the Red Corner; 'WHAT'S NEXT', comprising of Crucial Chris and Dangerous Dave. I shit you not; both high profile members of The Monster Raving Loony Party and both currently appearing onstage with the now legendary, but sadly no longer with us, CLANG! ... SCREAMING LORD SUTCH. Chris and Dave's social standing? Signing on. Intriguing I thought. You would never get away with it today but back in, hang on, Tottenham v Nottingham Forest, must have been 1991, it was doable. We all had a go for a while. I bottled out when playing a duo gig on a Tuesday night in Sunningdale and the man at the bar had a clipboard and was writing consistently through our set. Chris and I worryingly agreed he was from the tax office. I signed off. He didn't.

I started living in a room in a big house by the river in Wraysbury, not quite realising that it was also being used as Loony Party HQ. Before I realised quite how deep in I had dug myself, I was in a car on route to London at 6am, being told to just smile and wear a bowler hat and rosette. Forty minutes later I was sitting on Sky News, looking like some kind of local village idiot making his debut appearance on The Jeremy Kyle show! This had to change. How could I keep a foot in the blue and red corner? The answer? Different hats, same smile.

I only ever used the blue corner celebrity card once, and it wasn't Beatle related. I was seeing a girl at the time who had very posh parents. I always knew our lives wouldn't be spent together as one big posh happy family when the mother (can't remember her name, but I do know Gary Lineker scored in that cup final, so that probably says it all) said to me, 'So when will you be stopping this silly hobby and getting a proper job?' The clock was ticking. Just time to trump her when, out for dinner at a posh italian restaurant in Virginia Water, the mother announced very loudly after 6 double Gins, 'if you're supposed to be a musician how come you don't know anyone famous?' As the associated fellow poshies around the table laughed with her and at me, who should walk in, CLANG! ... RUSS ABBOTT. 'Hi Smiley, thanks for letting me get up and play your drums on Sunday mate, it was a great show and you're an awesome drummer.' That was mine and the mother's last supper together. Cheers blue corner.

Around this time I got my first real insight into the fine line between fame or bust. Two very handsome lads had started coming to our shows, blue and red corner, and being a bit younger and a lot handsomer sat wide-eyed and open mouthed at Zak's guitar solos and Crucial Chris's top hats. We shared a beer together one night and it transpired they were in a boyband called SLAMM who were signed to Pete Waterman's Rick Astley and Kylie Minogue led, giant label, PWL. Their schedule was insane. Jump in a van, drive 8 hours to Scotland to appear on stage at midnight to mime one song then drive home. The lads had a new single coming out. PWL saw them as the new Boyzone. Those lads. They were all set for super stardom. Johnny the singer and Scott the drummer. Top lads on the verge of mega-stardom.

Back in 1991 the singles chart dictated everything. There was the Wednesday midweek chart position and hopefully, with a few more midnight mimes, an added push up the chart, announced on Sunday night on Radio One by Mark Goodier. See, I remember that. Add to this the greatest carrot of them all ... Top of the Pops. The basic premise was this for Slamm; crack the Top Forty and, the following

Thursday, your now well rehearsed mime will be seen by eleven million viewers, of which about nine million will be girls who will want to sleep with you. So, Wednesday lunchtime. Scotts house. The whole band ready to leave for a midnight mime rendezvous in Darlington; and me, duo at the Dog and Fireside awaiting. There we all sat, nervously waiting for the PWL phone call re midweek chart posish. The phone rings. The ridiculously chiselled Scott picks up: 'Hi Scott speaking, uh huh, uh huh, uh huh, ok bye for now.' A pause. It's borderline amazing news. The lads are perched at number forty-three. This means with a final push in Dundee, Skegness, and G.A.Y. in London, Sunday's chart could be broken and Slamm will be the next big thing!!! The song stiffed at forty-one and they split up. Scott became a stunt man and Johnny now works for a record company. That, my friends, is the fine line between Boyzone and Let Loose.

## CHAPTER 3
## ... FASCINATIONS

I have always been fascinated by three things; hair loss, the ageing process and people watching. 'Why?' I hear you ask, about the second two, because those of you who know me may have realised that mother was right; dipping your fringe in fourteen gallons of peroxide will A; lighten the colour, B; help you look like you are on a yacht singing Rio in a pink suit, and C; you wont have a fringe very far into your thirties.

I can remember my first inquisitive look into the mirror at my friend Vicki's house, strange lighting if I remember rightly. There was definitely a little more forehead poking its little head through her sun kissed bathroom. Surely not. I asked Vicki. 'Noooooo' she replied, just like you do when you are cornered and have to tell a convincing whopper to get you out of jail. I started wearing a hat. I thought it was cool. It wasn't. It certainly wasn't on a stinkingly hot summer day when I pulled off my now minging orange woolly hat to the gasp of the, so called, friends in the dressing room. 'What the f**k's going on up there' was a particular memorable quote. 'It's all going a bit thin up there dude' was another belter, if I remember rightly, in that moment of shameful realisation that Michael Hutchence and I would never again be mistaken for each other because we had 'similar barnets'; I breathed a long, sad, breath and thought one thing: 'thank God Jain isn't here.' Knobhead!

It's a strange thing, hair loss. You start becoming obsessed with other people's crowns and quietly celebrate when you see a chink in their follicle armoury. Kerry tells me off all the time when I gleefully text her with a smiley face and the words 'old Pete's losing his barnet, kiss kiss, smiley face.' The reply usually consists of 'no he isn't, stop being a prick, no smiley face, one kiss'. I struggled for years to come to terms with it as I seemed to be the only one in the club. Everyone around me, apart from Trevor, was swanning around with long, shiny, thick locks. That's the other thing, this was right around the time when everyone had long hair, and cowboy boots, and waistcoats. Oh, hang on though, that may have been a bit before. Sadly, for me, it was more Jason Donovan than The Edge. Ok, I've checked. I still had hair during the Jase period which was 1989 (Liverpool 3 Everton 2). Yep, it was the early nineties that everyone started looking three inches above my eyeliner when engaging in conversation. I felt like a busty lady who never gets eye contact from a randy man!

So, I clung onto my longer hair look which, short of a comb over, gave me a bit of breathing space, but not much. I wanted to look like Kurt Cobain. The only similarity was the colour; the style was more Terry Nutkins. Its amazing isn't it how you genuinely can't see how stupid you look at the time, that everyone has 'he's losing his barnet' written all over their stupid faces but most of them, Cassell's and Speight's apart, would say nothing. So I cracked on in my own little Kurt Cobain/Terry Nutkins tribute world. It's easy nowadays because shaved heads are cool. My dear old friend Alan Thompson was on a similar follicle level to me a few years ago and would keep saying. 'If it's good enough for Jason Statham Smi, it's good enough for us.' Kind of where the similarities ended for me and the Stathe I think, although I'm a better actor than he is. So now looking back from my fifty-one years on the planet, I like to be a wise old hair owl, sharing my wisdom to the future follically challenged. 'Bone it mate' basically means getting the clippers out and shaving off the small amount of hair you had left, always followed by the positive 'Statham' example. So you will see for yourself in the pictures in the book that it was a gradual process till my dear friend Jen, nearly on a par with Jain in the piss taking stakes but not quite (Jain will never be beaten bless her) told me that I had a great face for a shaved head. I was lucky she said, not everyone had a crown shaped like mine, not everyone had cheekbones crying out for a grade one to shelter under. Then she pulled out the clippers and before I could say 'just a little bit off the sides please love', it was gone. Did I feel rejuvenated? Like a man reborn ready to face the world with a marvellous crown and tremendous cheek bones? Nope, I hated it, but it was a bit late by then and when I saw Jain and she said, without a smirk in sight, "That's better, you don't look like a knobhead any more", the future was bright, the future was grade one.

People watching is another fascination of mine. I think one of the reasons is that, doing what I do for a living, I'm only one of maybe four or five people who get to see what we do. You see sitting behind a drum kit looking out into the crowd, everyone else is looking in my direction, so in a crowd of say a thousand, that's a pretty sizeable ratio in my lap for seeing stuff no one, apart from the others on the stage, will see. Things like air punching. What's that all about? Thrusting your right arm skywards in perfect tandem to my kick drum. You wouldn't do it in Tesco if they popped a bit of S Club 7 over the tannoy would you? Hang on, I actually know some who would, but it's still a bonkers thing to do; as is the 'secret grope'. The cheeky side on tactic used by gentlemen who have lucked out and been popped next to a lovely looking lady, lost in the words and melody of a hymn being sung directly to her (in her world), and, probably, nine hundred and ninety nine others; but in her world, just to her. So from my observational birds nest I can see what you cant, the cheeky chancers who think 'she's loving this moment so much, I wonder if she would like to enhance it with some physical interaction', or as its also known, a cheeky grope. Subtle at first if they are seasoned professionals, steady as we go, we are only in the first verse. Maybe a subtle arm around the cup of the back, just to add to the euphoria of the upcoming chorus, middle eight and guitar solo. Chorus one; they have moved the cupping across into arm around the waist territory. She is in her element. Not only are the words being sung just for her by the colossus of music magnetism on the stage but, in his world she is now experiencing a super groovy kind of physical attraction. The solo is coming ... The second chorus is close to climax. Her head goes back. She screams with delight as, in perfect tandem, the 56 Les Paul Custom hits a melting D minor chord followed by a note lingering in the air, like a helium ballon let go by a child at a fete an hour previously. NOW! He goes for the kill. It's his moment; her moment; their moment. He moves his waist clutching right hand and cups her 34DD right bosom. She freezes. As the solo crashes into the final chorus, she pulls her 34DD away from the clutching grip and goes to the bar. Close but no cigar. He simply shrugs and moves to his left in search of the next contender. I swear I have seen this so many times, usually when, CLANG! ... ROBBIE WILLIAMS, is cracking out the final 'and through it alllllll'. It's a spectator sport I wish you could all partake in but, sadly, exclusive to drummers on big risers.

As for the ageing process. Facebook was a revelation but not as instantly gratifying as Friends Reunited. Remember that? You could look up all the old faces you hadn't kept in touch with from those crazy old days at Kenyngton Manor. Countless hours were lost perusing pictures of people I never liked who never liked me who now had no hair (HURRAH), wrinkles, and were about 3 stone heavier; and that was just the girls (sorry, couldn't resist that one). Yes the ageing process is a fascinating thing. Don't get me wrong, I don't trawl through pictures of people who were four foot seven the last time I saw them and delight that they are now bald and fat, I just find the whole process so interesting.

So, back in 2016 (Man Utd V Crystal Palace, a 2-1 victory remembered mostly for Palace manager Alan Pardew's ridiculous Dad dance when Palace opened the scoring). Anyway, that's how I remember it was 2016. I got a Facebook message inviting me to a school reunion. Not just a reunion, it was billed as the 30 coolest people from the Kenyngton Manor Class of '84. My first reaction was that I would rather stick pins in my eyes than spend a night with a bunch of people who I hadn't seen since the aforementioned 1984 and that there was probably a good reason for that. I had waved goodbye to Luther Vandross and headed East to the world of confused fashion and awesome music. My jeans and their jeans just didn't match. My boots and their boots were living in different postcodes, and as for the hair, they had side partings and perms at the back where I was still sporting my various blonde elements of peroxide fringeness. I wasn't up for it. I would obviously be far too busy in my new found world of Rock & Roll and, if not, then I'd probably be baby sitting. That's how I now rolled.

Anyway, two days before the second coming of the 84er's, Kerry informed me that she and Lola were going away for the weekend. My first thought, 'a weekend on the sofa with the dog in my pants eating crisps and watching footy'. My second thought, 'I'm gigging Friday night anyway'. Then a bizarre twist of fate. A phone call informing me that said gig was unavoidably cancelled. Mmm, and no footy or pants/crisps combo til Saturday lunchtime. Surely the heavens weren't sending me a sign to go meet my fellow pubetiers. The other twenty-nine coolest cats who I don't particularly remember being particularly cool, unless you were an Imagination fan. I looked at the dog. He looked at me. 'You should go' he said, in his Boxer voice. 'You think?' I replied. I was talking to a twelve-year-old Boxer dog!

So, the Friday evening came, and Kerry and Lola packed up and shipped off to one of her infamous family occasions (I am still scarred from the first and last experience). Love 'em. So, at eight thirty I am pacing the kitchen wondering if The Magpie pub in Sunbury is really a good option; to see all the lads; the girls. 'I know' I thought, 'I'll try to recall some names, the obvious ones'. I stopped counting at seven. 'What about if I drive over there and feel the vibe?' I looked at the dog. 'What's the worst that can happen?' he said, with his eyes. Who was I to argue with a Boxer? I drove to Sunbury. I was forty-eight years old. I had played stadiums around the world to thousands of people. At that moment in the Magpie car park I was more nervous than I was playing the Stade de France in Paris counting in the first song in front of 80,000 Muse fans. What connection had I had over the last 40 years? A couple of the lads were huge Jam fans and had tapped me up for From The Jam tickets. We had briefly met afterwards, and they had been extremely friendly. Two down, twenty-seven to go. I got out of the car and walked toward the door. The voice in my head (not the dogs) was saying, over and over again; 'they hated you at school'. Time to run away surely?, but this was a one off chance to see the age process at close quarters, to count first hand how many lads had lost their hair. All my favourite things in one room. In the words of Ant and Dec, I summoned up an enormous gulp of courage and mouthed the immortal lines 'lets get ready, lets get ready, lets get ready to rumble. Psych. Watch us wreck the mic.'

I used the classic left foot right foot combination and walked through the door. Twenty-nine ageing faces, half with no hair looked over in my direction. 'Yes, he's here' echoed around the room. I turned and looked around to see who they were greeting. No one behind me, and suddenly three bald Jam fans in front of me. 'Can't believe you came.' What a wonderful welcome. 'Drinks are on me' said Phillip, the mischievous fella at school who now owned five houses in five countries and was worth millions. A wave from some distantly familiar looking female faces, whose names were on the tip of my tongue. This was going well. Really well. A few more nods of appreciation headed my way from at least five guys who hated me at school. This was surreal. I got handed a beer and was suddenly surrounded by eight of the twenty-nine; all looking at me wide-eyed and inquisitively. 'So?' the first voice said. (Jamie; lived down my road when we were kids; nice mum who used to bake lovely fairy cakes in the holidays.)

'What's he like?' I looked at him and the fourteen other eyes now boring into my skull. 'Who?' I replied. Eight voices, in perfect unison, in perfect harmony, responded. 'ROBBIE!!!' Yes folks. They hadn't invited Smiley, or little Stevie B, who used to share chemistry lessons, and play up front in the school team. They had invited Robbie's drummer. The guy who they had seen sitting behind Britain's Top Pop picker, belting out Angels on Top Of The Pops, ably backed by their best friend at school.

The questions that followed really set the tone. 'So, how many houses have you got?' Neville; hated me at school; hit me once, straight in the face, with a basketball. 'Roughly?' I answered, 'One'. 'What are you driving? Merc? No, Jag? No, it's gotta be a Porsche?'. Lawrence; who had also lived down my road and got me kicked out of the Scouts, aged thirteen, for kissing a girl in the woods when we were supposed to bivouacking (she was my girlfriend and had brought me some sandwiches, bless her). 'Driving? I answered, 'er, Ford Focus.' The room went very quiet. Neville, Jamie and Lawrence looked disappointingly at each other and stood up, grabbed their Fosters, and walked to the other side of the room.

I sat alone for about a minute planning my exit, when Big Liam sauntered across. He was six foot three at school, shaving before I'd grown a single pube. He sat down, slightly pickled. He was still six foot three. 'I want to thank you.' he said. 'Really? Why's that then?' 'Because I reckon I got laid at least ten times because of you.' Fame comes in strange shapes and sizes my friends. This was possibly the strangest of all shapes and, indeed, sizes. I said goodbye. No one cared. I'd shattered all their illusions. I got in the Focus, started the engine, and Robbie's drummer drove home, to his dog, his crisps, and his footy, in his pants.

## CHAPTER 4
## ... WHEN TV GOES WRONG

Now I'm a musician; so, what's the next step? TV BABY!!!! The natural next rung on the showbiz ladder. From the audio to the visual. Let's face it, everybody loves a bit of telly, however tenuous. I've known people who have been an extra on Eastenders for 1.4 milliseconds who have already written their Bafta award speech. There's a country mile between the words Actor and Extra but in the eye of the beholder you are still on telly, and people love you for it, even when you make a complete donkey of yourself in front of eleven million viewers on prime time ITV Saturday night telly. My first, and most disastrous folly into Bafta territory was on that classic light entertainment juggernaut YOU BET, hosted by the charmingly bearded, CLANG! ... MATTHEW KELLY.

I had received a call from an old friend of mine who was working as a researcher on the show. 'Could you hit a hundred snare drums in under a minute?' I put her on hold, went and grabbed some sticks, and played four hundred single strokes. Fifty-seven seconds. 'Just.' I said. 'Perfect!' she replied, and said they would be in touch. Sure enough, the call came and two weeks weeks later I was on route to Shepperton Studios, with my new housemate Aussie Mick, to rehearse for that evening's show. I had even managed to blag thirty tickets for friends and family and, after two weeks of making sure that anyone within a fifty mile radius knew that I was gonna be on the telly, it was shaping up to be quite an event. What could possibly go wrong? I've since learned, with hindsight, that what you wear on telly can seriously come back to haunt you. In fact, that particular episode of You Bet popped its little head up fairly recently, on UK Gold, thirty odd years later. A friend called me to say they had recorded it. I offered cash straight away for them to bury it. Best twenty-five quid I've ever spent. Anyway, back to Shepperton Studios, where me and the Aussie are ushered in to a huge studio containing 100 snare drums all in a huge circle and in perfect symmetry. I was briefed as to the concept. Basically the challenge was to run around the hundred drums hitting each one four times in under a minute. The celebrity panel were so famous that I genuinely can't remember who all of them were. CLANG! ... ANNABELLE GILES, I think was one, but as for the other two, there was probably a Doctor Fox or a Darren Day in there somewhere too; my infamous memory has, however, erased that info. So, the first run through. Three, two, one. BOOM! Fifty-seven seconds. A small smattering of applause from people with clipboards and polystyrene tea cups, and a non-arsed nod of approval from the Aussie. Camera rehearsal. Three, two, one. BOOM! Fifty-four seconds. Hang on, this is all getting a bit easy. A researcher came over and whispered in my ear. 'Try not to do it too quickly, anything between fifty-seven and fifty-nine would be perfect.' 'I could pop the brakes on around snare number thirty-six I think, to raise the tension levels.' We established this as a good plan. We were good to go.

Showtime, just about two hours away, in front of a live audience. What could possibly go wrong? Where's my pen. 'First of all, I'd like to thank Bafta for this award ...' So, what to wear? Now I was still in and around the Jason Donavan 'Too Many Broken Hearts' era, so it was all cowboy boots, long flowing blonde hair and, uh oh, waistcoats.

I recall the waistcoat memory with an 'Uh oh' because I once went on a date and when I was shown into the lounge of my date's parent's house, my waistcoat was the exact same colour and pattern of their sofa and curtains. A soft furnishing fashion nightmare scenario I know you've probably all encountered. No? Just me then.

Anyway, back to the dressing room, where Aussie Mick and I are passing the time in the way that we always did, whenever we weren't watching re runs of Cheers, BACKGAMMON. This would be a big part of my future musical life and I had been taught by the master. The Jackie Chan of the double. Aussie Mick was a great teacher, and, being stoned off his face half the time, was totally up for putting in the hours, just as long as there was a healthy stash of Monster Munch crisps at arm's length. So as the master and his young apprentice were throwing double sixes in the dressing room with SMILEY written inside a big gold star on the door, in came the bubbly genial host himself. Full of beans and gin and tonics wishing me luck. 'You're on after the guy with the german shepherd.' That's showbiz.

Twenty minutes later, a knock at the door and we were ready to go. Now, I'd got a pair of sticks in my hand and a spare in both back pockets of my recently purchased ripped jeans. Suddenly, new feelings appeared inside me. Butterflies, complete with sweaty palms, very sweaty palms ... I had never experienced this sensation before. It was quite unnerving. The german shepherd has completed his task of juggling 18 footballs on one paw and we are heading to a commercial break. The butterflies are really stirring me up. I was sweating like Jimmy Saville in Toys R Us. It was all feeling quite weird when, suddenly, I heard, 'WILL YOU WELCOME STEVE SMILEY BARNARD!!!' Bam. The doors opened. Music played. Applause. A few wolf whistles from a couple of my guests. Matthew Kelly standing with his arms open like my favourite uncle at a family wedding. It went quiet. Uncle Matthew asked me a few questions. I nervously tried to answer, in that stupid way I do when I get nervous, which is basically humour, only funny to me (plenty more examples of that in this book if you stick with it). Matthew describes the challenge to the celebrity panel and the watching eleven million viewers, at least two of whom are sat in their lounge at home saying to each other 'his waistcoat matches our curtains.' Annabelle assures the audience that I will be a massive success. Doctor Fox, who isn't a real doctor or a real fox, isn't so sure and sits on the fence. The other fella says 'no chance', and that dear friends is where my memory of the next seven minutes evaporates. Suffice to say I dropped two sticks in the first ten seconds, as my hands were sweating with the weight of Annabelle's confidence, and I completely f****d it up. Thank goodness Gogglebox wasn't on back in the nineties.

Now if I told you I had an even better telly incident would you believe me? Not quite as disastrous, but by this point I was cool. I had it going on. It was many years later and I got a call to sit in with the house band on Channel 4's Late Lunch, presented by the mighty, CLANG! ... MEL AND SUE, pre-Bake Off. It was a great show which I watched regularly at 6pm on a Friday evening. When I arrived in the afternoon, I found out two things. The first being that there were twenty-five short bursts of music on totally live telly. The theme tune, into the commercial breaks, out of the commercial breaks, and during the show, all of which instigated by me, the drummer, but without the use of the usual one two three four count in. No, this was live telly and I was taught a host of strangely named drum fills to introduce each song. 'Flats in Dagenham', a snare and tom combo to introduce the show. Then varying intros including snare and kick combo 'Sherbet Dib Dab', 'Billy Billy Billy Billy' on the snare, and my new favourite tom and snare combo 'It Ain't Arf Hot Mum'.

The second thing I found out was awesome. The guests. Surely it couldn't get any better than this. CLANG! ... THE CAST OF MEN BEHAVING BADLY. Yep, the Lovely, CLANG! ... LESLIE ASH, before she messed with her lips; together with CLANG! ... MARTIN CLUNES; CLANG! ... NEIL MORRISEY; and CLANG! ... CAROLINE QUENTIN. I loved that show, and Tony and Gary very much mirrored me and Aussie Mick in our laziest heyday. Ding dong merrily on high. Have I mentioned that it was the 23rd of December? Have I mentioned that it was the Christmas show?, and have I mentioned that I had told every single living soul I'd ever met in my lifetime that I was gonna be on live telly at 6pm?

So, at 5.45 I was asked to go to the wardrobe department. Myself and the band walked in, and there were the whole 'Behaving Badly' gang; all very pleasant; and all slightly pissed; but all seemingly having a secret giggle with each other. After we were all introduced and with only ten minutes to go before my second Bafta winning performance, the now immortal lines were announced. 'Do you want to come and get into your costumes?' Costumes? First time I had heard that word all day. I discovered that Caroline Quentin actually snorts when she laughs, when behind us, hanging on the wall, while the ghetto blaster was playing 'Jingle All The Way', were 4 ELF

OUTFITS, complete with matching red pointy hats and boots. Leslie Ash's pre collagen lips were wide with elf appreciation. Tony and Gary just shot a look of 'Bet you wish you hadn't told all your friends elf boy' and Mel and Sue giggled like they would twenty years later when some poor baker's 'banana and custard sponge' had toppled over during one of Paul and Mary's tasting sessions.

So, at six o'clock, everyone I knew in the world heard channel 4's snare and tom combo of 'Flats in Dagenham'. The cameras moved slowly around the audience members, loudly shouting and applauding, and eight seconds later the camera was pointing at four elves in pointy red hats playing 'It's Late Lunch', homing in on the poor drummer elf trying to play 4/4 beat, in matching pointy red elf hat and boots.

Television can be a cruel mistress sometimes, especially when you're wearing an elf outfit, or something that matches your curtains.

## CHAPTER 5
## ... CAN U DIG IT?

'Can you understand me now.' The opening line to the best pop song ever written. It's 1992 and Can U Dig It by The Mock Turtles is being playing on the radio. A lot. It's the best pop song ever. Starting with a killer guitar riff, then the band kick in with the coolest bass line walking up its fretboard, a haunting vocal over a transient hammond organ and dandy drum pattern and within thirty seconds the most killer of all chorus hooks, CAN U DIG IIIT OH YEAH!!! sung at top volume by me every time it was played on Radio One. I'm driving around in my white Peugeot 205 van, the perfect vehicle for a man with a black Pearl drum kit now playing six nights a week in pubs, clubs, weddings, christenings, barmitzvahs and school fetes. You name it, I drummed at it.

I'd branched out a bit musically into blues bands; I couldn't name them, and neither could you for that matter, but they were busy playing gigs in back room bars on Tuesday & Wednesday evenings. Tricky nights to fill generally unless you're on tour, but I wasn't there yet so these were handy diary fillers. One such evening was in a back room bar in Teddington, I genuinely can't remember the band, I think Jeff and Doctor Richard may have been on guitar and bass duties, and Noel or Dunken, with a K, were probably singing and blowing into harmonicas every sixty fourth bar. Funny thing the blues. Really samey, like jazz, but if you climb inside it and shut your eyes 'Hoochie Coochie Man' doesn't sound quite the same as 'Roadhouse Blues.' Ha ha, who am I trying to kid. They all sound the same. I didn't even bother looking at the set list. There were only two types of blues. Fast or slow. Jeff would tip me off and away we would go.

So, on this wet Wednesday night in Teddington a SLIDING DOOR MOMENT happened. After the eighth slow and ninth fast blues song, with harmonica solo, I went into the toilet for a wee. As I stood reflecting on the fast/slowness of the previous hour the man next to me, doing the same but probably not thinking the same, said 'You're impressing some pretty important people'. 'Really?' I replied, wondering which Howling Wolf fan had liked which particularly slow version of 'Crossroads' we had just drawn out for twelve minutes. 'Have you heard of a band called The Mock Turtles?' said legendary producer, CLANG! ... PETE SMITH. He famously produced Sting and, currently, the Manchester band I had listened to in the Peugeot for the past 3 weeks and loved since I first heard that opening line. 'The singer wants to meet you.' That would be the singer, the incredibly cool, CLANG! ... MARTIN COOGAN, brother of Steve, and who I had witnessed the night before on Top Of The Pops resplendent in sky blue jacket and matching jeans.

Pete led me toward the back of the room and said, 'Martin, this is Smiley.' He turned around and smiled, resplendent in sky blue jacket and matching jeans. The old nervous mist came over me like a predictable autumnal shower. 'Didn't you wear that on Top of the Pops?' was my ridiculous opening gambit to the coolest man I'd ever met. 'Well I haven't really been to bed since.' replied still the coolest man I'd ever met. The autumnal shower stopped pouring and we began to chat. 'This should be your drummer Martin.' said Pete. 'Would you be up to moving to Manchester to join my band?' asked Martin. Just as he said it Doctor Richard, a bass playing Doctor, in medieval history, not medicine, beckoned me back to the stage for another fast or slow rendition of the same song I had played for the last hour. Martin assured me he would stay till the end, no matter how many trips to the gents he had to make, and true to his word, and his bladder, we finished our conversation an hour later, wide-eyed and bushy-tailed (him not me). He informed me that the band were in the studio making their second album and, as much as he wanted me to be an instant Turtle, the current drummer was still inhabiting the Turtle drum stool. He would put the option to the vote when he finally got back to the studio, and finally changed his clothes. It took a year (not to change his clothes). We kept in contact during those 12 months, with lots of promises and plans, and, at half time during the 1993 cup final (Liverpool v Sunderland) in my Mum and Dad's lounge, I was asked to join The Mock Turtles.

To be honest, I wasn't very well travelled back in 1993. So Manchester sounded a bit daunting. Luckily for me, Dangerous Dave had an uncle in that part of Lancashire and offered to drive me; yes, that Dave. He drove me in full Monster Raving Loony costume. We got to Martin's house and knocked on the door. He answered the door with a confused double take, and then we all went into the kitchen to meet Martyn Glynn Murray, the guitarist. (Do you remember the episode of Gavin and Stacey, the one where they got married. MGM played the photographer who just kept saying 'Crackin' over and over again.) He also gave a strange double take reaction to his new drummer and the guy in full Limahl style wig, kilt, and cowboy boot, combo. I got rid of Dave asap and MGM did say his heart had sunk when he first set eyes on his new Kajagoogoo lookalike drummer. Luckily now it was just me in a

Martin sandwich and we chewed the Mancunian fat before leaving for rehearsals. When we arrived there was Andy Stewardson, six foot three, and as calm and cool a bassist as you will ever meet. Then in walked Jo Gent. Instantly lovely, and after a Yorkshire tea it was time to play. Cue killer guitar riff, and all into the best pop song ever. I was now a Mock Turtle. Elaine Constantine who later directed the fantastic Northern Soul film, was a friend of the band, and happened to have a spare room in her house in North Manchester; so after a week at home getting my bits together, me and the Peugeot moved to 'Up North'.

The band was now being managed by the same company as James. They were huge at the time with 'Sit Down' riding high in the charts, and they had big funky offices and killer merchandise. Do you remember the flower t-shirts? Well a week later everyone in Wraysbury was wearing one as they had uttered the dangerous words to a cheeky southern drummer 'Help yourself to as much merch as you like'. That's what it sounded like anyway, the same as it did years later in The Alarm world.

The next two weeks were spent rehearsing and looking in the NME for the big announcement about the new Mock Turtles drummer. I'm still waiting. The plan was for an eight date UK tour. My first tour. It was the little things that really stood out for me on that first tour. Getting into a posh splitter bus, with posh seats, with the rest of the band rather than travelling alone in the trusty Peugeot. Being able to have a second pint, and third and fourth after a show (they know how to drink those northerners); and getting a laminated pass, with those magic three big black letters... AAA, ACCESS ALL AREAS. The holy grail for any musician, and for fans, usually only obtained by theft or getting the musician far too drunk and him becoming very generous in a drunken moment of weakness. That's a red card in musician world. It was ace. With a pass around my neck and a new Pearl MLX kit, courtesy of the band, we headed towards our first show, at The Boardwalk in Manchester. If you're now stroking your chin and thinking you've heard of that venue before, it's famous for being where Oasis were first born and rehearsed themselves into the band we all grew to love. The evening was mind blowing and I realised there and then that touring was definitely the life for me. A few shows later, we played in Sheffield. The support band were amazing, really young but so good. They were called The Jennifers, but soon afterward they changed their name to, CLANG! ... SUPERGRASS.

The next show was a real eye opener to the new boy on drums, the London Show. In later years these would be known as the nightmare shows, due to the mythical Holy Grail known as The Guest List. That's right friends, the Guest List. A handy and impressive tool used in far away towns where you may know one or two people, to invite them to your show and catch up before, and indeed afterwards, whilst in between showing them how well your musical life is going. Yes, in distant towns and cities The List is a handy social tool. In London it's an utter nightmare. You see, contrary to popular belief, we the musicians are only given a select number of spaces on the magic list. It's like having to list your children, friends and family in order of popularity. Most understand. Some don't, some really don't. I've lost friends over the years who I've had to say no to. Were they real friends then? I hear you ask. Not any more they're not.

CLANG! ... STEVE COOGAN, was an ever present at his older brother's gigs. Ironically Steve is, in my opinion, the third funniest Coogan, behind Martin and Brendan. He was an intriguing character. He would often listen to conversations and when you said something funny he wouldn't laugh with everyone else, he would smirk and say 'I like that', like he was making a mental note of your hilariously delivered cockney gag. I'm sure I once said AHA!!! In front of Steve, coincidence? You'll have to ask Alan. We played at a cool club in London one night and I found myself sat between Steve and, CLANG! ... JOHN THOMPSON. Now that was funny.

Sadly, around this time, when the band should have catapulted into the pop stratosphere, their record company was being bought out and they were shoved onto another label, who didn't really dig it, excuse the pun. So the band drifted for many years until, in 2003 I think, (let me check, yes Arsenal v Southampton) Vodafone picked up the best pop song ever and started using it on their ad campaign on the TV and radio, and The Mock Turtles were re-born. The single was remixed by, CLANG! ... FATBOY SLIM, and we were asked to do Top Of The Pops and then, the following morning, TV AM. At this point bands on Top Of The Pops were often playing live, not like my future miming adventures, that will come to a head later in the book, if you haven't found anything better to do by then and are still persevering with it. So, it was quite a challenge and a little bit nerve wracking. I remember we were on first and also remember the panic of not being able to hear Martins guitar intro. Within a five second moment I had panicked, thought about stopping Top Of the Pops and re-starting the song. I didn't, thankfully. That would have been career suicide. I took a wild guess and got lucky. I remember being awful in that three-and-a-half-minute TV appearance. I don't know why. Everything I had learned up until that moment about poise, groove, swing and technique went out of the window. No one ever mentioned it to me so maybe it was my paranoia, or me recalling past TV disasters.

After the show we stayed in London and got a teeny weeny bit drunk, not that big a deal, unless you are appearing on TV AM the next morning and your wake up call is 4:45am. The make up department put in an extra shift making us look spritely and full of breakfast telly beans and we mimed our way through with, CLANG! ... PENNY SMITH, singing along, before telling us all what the weather had in store that day. Coogan had a massive crush on her. I'd met her in make-up and told her, and she duly agreed to pop her head in our dressing room to inform me that she had left some of her underwear in my room the night before, and could she please have it back, in front of an open mouthed Coogan brother. They are lively those weather girls, and certainly game for a laugh. Didn't Ulrika Jonsson used to be a weather girl? I rest my case.

Sadly, after a couple more TV appearances, one notable for the presenter taking the piss out of fellow guest, CLANG! ... MIDGE URE, who then walked off, mid show; and another with, CLANG! ... Zoe Ball, which I remember being brilliant, that was kind of it for the fabulous MT's. Still one of my favourite bands, I still meet up with Martin or Jo whenever I am up north. Will we ever do anything again? I doubt it but hey, stranger things have happened, or been said. AAAHHHHHAAAAAAAAA.

## CHAPTER 6
## ... THE BIG BREAK(fast)

So, it's now about 1996. It's the summer of love. The year before, 1995, Oasis and Blur had had a right old ding dong over a 'Country House'; and the year after, 1997, Tony Blair became our, guitar playing, friend of the stars, all round top bloke, Prime Minister, before he became a war criminal of course. No, this is 1996, and all you can hear in the pubs, cars and offices is 'It's coming home, it's coming home ... football's coming home!!' It was the feel-good year of all feel-good years.

I was still diversifying my drumming talents into even more whacky shapes. This time I was on a 60's nostalgia tour in Germany, playing and singing for old Uncle Len and The Tremeloes. It was amazing. All these older, wrinklier, balder, versions of the 60's and 70's Top Of The Pops re-runs on UK Gold. The ones you don't see now cos Uncle Jimmy Sav was presenting and, clearly, he only had one eye, and hand for that matter, on the show. All the bands I grew up listening to when I was really young were on the bill. The Sweet, with, CLANG! ... BRIAN CONNOLLY. He could hardly stand up by this point and had to be ushered to the mic by a younger, similar looking, man, who then sat at the back of the stage, and sang all the songs while Brian mimed, then shuffled him off again. Tragic to see. Then there was The Bay City Rollers. Still fronted by the still youthful looking, CLANG! ... LES McKEWEN. I thought I would break the ice with Les in catering one day while queueing for a sausage. The conversation went like this. 'Hello Les, I just wanted to say thank you. It was down to you that I learnt to play drums whilst growing up and playing along to your songs.' I thought that would make him feel good. I was wrong. 'Are you saying I'm f****n old?!!!' was his wide-eyed Glasgow retort. The last chat we had as I recall.

I did meet some brilliant old pros on that tour. The Searchers, Dozy Beaky Mick &, the 6ft 5, Titch, and The Swinging Blue Jeans. All well up for sharing tales of the 60's and 70's if you were up for getting the beers in. After the German trip, Uncle Len led his new young Tremeloes out to Egypt for two shows. This included an early morning horse ride out to the pyramids to watch the sun come up. It was an incredible moment. If you've been to Egypt, were you surprised at how small the Sphynx is in real life? I was.

Anyway, Silence was Golden and it was back to the six nights a week shlepping around gigging. I had branched out again by starting to do duo and trio gigs with local legends Chris and Flick. This consisted of them on acoustic guitars, a tambourine, three stools, with me sat in the middle singing. They were easy gigs. A load of Oasis songs sung loudly back at us with me sitting in the middle thinking I was Liam Gallagher but probably looking and sounding more like Liam Neeson. 'I will find you and I will kill you, cos you're my wonderwall.'

One night we were driving home late. I was on steering duty now in an old white Fiat Uno. I had smashed the Peugeot on New Years Eve coming round the corner from the M4 to the M25. It was cold and foggy, and two cars had crashed a hundred yards ahead. As soon as I saw them I slammed on the brakes, then slid sideways for what seemed like ages, like a slow motion scene out of the Matrix (probably three seconds but felt like twenty), and smashed sideways into one of the already crashed cars. In the silence that was the next few moments I looked down and saw blood all over my left hand and leg. I wiped my hand across my face and staggered out of the obliterated Peugeot. 'Can't believe you just smashed into my already pre-smashed car' said some fat obnoxious knobhead who I was about to punch square in the face when a policeman came and sat me on the barrier, agreeing with my knobhead judgement. It was now snowing, and I was freezing. An ambulance came. My first and last ride in one. They are quite fun actually. They asked who they should ring to tell them I was on the way to Ashford Hospital. I was 28 years old. I was a musician. A man of the world. So, after they had phoned my Mum, she came, with my Dad, to pick me up from Ashford Hospital. I was sitting in a wheelchair when they walked in, with bloodstained jeans and shirt. The look of horror on her face lives with me to this day. Mum recalls it well because, what she initially saw was her little boy with a six-inch gash running from cheek to cheek. Her precious little boy now scarred for life. It was only when she took three steps closer that she did that thing only Mums can do. She licked her handkerchief and wiped the dried blood which I'd wiped across my face to reveal my youthful good looks still intact. If I've over dramatised that episode of Casualty I apologise, but I've got a book to sell!

So back to the new gig wagon, and the newly named Chris Flick & Smiley (that must have been a long meeting). One particular night, we were driving down the A30 in Camberley when a blue light appears in the Uno rear view mirror. We pulled up and the police car pulled over in front of us. I reassured the chaps that I haven't been drinking and that I was insured and taxed to the max, so I would simply charm the policewoman, who had now appeared from the car, and we'd be on our merry trio way. As I got out to begin my charm offensive, I suddenly realised that the policewoman in front of me was my old friend Alison, who I hadn't seen for years. After she pointed out my left brake light was faulty, we had a quick catch up and she asked who was in the impressive Uno. I explained that there were two members of the now infamous CF&S and she asked if I fancied a bit of a wind up. She was always very funny and had regularly taken piss taking to a near Jain standard back in the day. Now, who was I to deny her a little wind up fun, so dutifully agreed. She then turned me around and made me put my hands on the car bonnet. After slowly running her hands up and down my chest and gently squeezing my buttocks, she turned me back around and planted a slow lingering kiss on me, in front of two opened mouthed trioists. She then winked, put a piece of paper in my hand and after whooshing her hair Charlies Angels stylee, smiled, coyly bit her lip, and waved me goodbye. When I got back in the car there was a deathly silence. I think that's what you call the long arm of the law. Cheeky minx.

Another memorable evening was when Crucial Chris and I were on our way back from a gig in a car we had borrowed form our mate Dunken, as the Uno was being fixed, again. As we were heading back along the M3 we both noticed a bit of smoke coming from the engine and the car losing power. We decided to pull off the motorway at the next junction and, as we did, so the car juddered to a halt. Suddenly, the smoke started coming thicker and more urgently from the engine and we made the executive decision to get out. Now neither Chris nor I were what you would call mechanically minded, and one of us was pretty stoned. We decided to open the bonnet. In hindsight not the best decision. As we did so the car burst into flames. The stoned one and I looked at each other, then dived into the back of the car to get all the equipment out. Like a couple of roadies nearing dinner time, we had everything out and on the grass verge just as the Vauxhall Cavalier Estate was engulfed in flames. We stood in the neon glow of burning car as we heard a siren in the distance. As Dunken's car was heading for fire and theft territory a fire engine swung around the corner and pulled next to the now gathering crowd. Five minutes later after some pretty impressive hose action, the fire was out, as was Dunken's car, for the count. Dunk actually took the situation very well for a man who had lent his car to a mate who thought he had insurance but didn't. We are still friends, although he did emigrate to New Zealand. Coincidence? Surely not...

Around this time, I had joined some session agencies. This was tricky back in the day as my CV wasn't what you would call, spectacular. Screaming Lord Sutch, The Tremeloes and You Bet was hardly ELO and Take That, so the phone wasn't running hot with 'A' list auditions. Then out of the blue I did receive a call from one of the agencies, asking if I would be up for playing drums the next morning on the Big Breakfast. Now I loved that show. It was being presented by, CLANG! ... JOHNNY VAUGHAN, who is still one of my favourite TV/Radio personalities. So I was well up for it. All I had to do was take my kit and turn up at the studios over the other side of East London at 5:30am the next morning. This was it. Breakfast telly. The cool one. This would be great. None of your You Bet nonsense. No elf outfits. Just my drums, me, five million viewers, and, as I found out at 5:29 that following morning, ninety-nine other drummers, all participating in trying to break the world record for most drummers on a breakfast show. Not quite what I had envisaged but hey, I was here now.

Bizarrely, in amongst the plethora of wham bammers, a kind of SLIDING DOOR MOMENT came courtesy of my bass drum. It was sporting a hand painted brightly coloured swirly pattern and the producers decided that should be front row middle of all the other noisy buggers. They also decided to interview two of the hundred. I was on Johnny's left and a ridiculously handsome chap stood to his right. I remember two things about that morning. 1; Oasis had just gone to number one with 'Some Might Say' as was joyously announced live on the show, and, 2; CLANG! ... NATALIE IMBRUGLIA, was the co-host. She was absolutely stunning. I probably said something nervously stupid to her. Just a hunch.

Anyway, as we come back form the adverts Johnny introduces a hundred drummers all sitting behind their kits, sticks in hand, all ready to get on a future episode of Record Breakers with Norris McWhirter. John (we were on first named terms by now) stood between me and Richard, the handsome one. 'So, tell me who you drum for man?' John asked. 'Gary Numan' replied Rich. Please don't ask me that question, how could I possibly choose between a monster raving loony and a Tremeloe. He didn't ask. He just said, 'Are you ready to rock?'. 'Yes.' I said, with poise, confidence and just a hint of swagger. Then, two hundred arms belonging to blokes with pieces of wood in their hands proceeded to make a noise resembling five hundred drunken tap dancers falling down eight flights of stairs, in tutu's. No reason for the tutu bit, but it adds a bit of colour. I knew there and then that my CV needed some serious upgrading. Another SLIDING DOOR was about to... slide open.

## CHAPTER 7
## ... EAST 17

Session agencies are like buses. You get nothing and then you get, well, two come along, but this one was rather different. The agency who had called about the big brekkie were looking for two drummers to play with a little-known UK rap act called JPAC. Never heard of them? Nor had I. The agency had obviously been impressed with Richard, and his 'Gary Numan' response, and my fabulous delivery of the word 'Yes,' on live breakfast telly, enough to know they had the perfect boys for the job. The interesting bit of the conversation was the next bit. JPAC were one of the support acts on the upcoming, CLANG! ... EAST 17, six-week Arena tour of the UK and Europe. Wow! Rehearsals began in three days in London.

I wanted to celebrate but it was Monday night, which was five a side football night. I got my kit on and headed to the leisure centre. Twenty minutes later I was on my way to A&E with a suspected fractured elbow. Didn't even get a penalty. Come on ref! The x-ray showed a hairline fracture. Was I going to sit at home in plaster for five weeks looking like I was about to enter an arm-wrestling tournament? Noooooo. I had a tour to go on, so I made my excuses and slipped out of St Peter's Hospital. My Mum was a bit concerned when I told her but after a brief consultation with my Auntie Mary who was a nurse, it was agreed that I should crack on (excuse the pun).

That briefly reminds me of when I was living in a flat by the River Thames, in the Staines massive, a few years previously, with a bloke called Ant. I'd kind of been lumbered with Ant as he was a friend of Aussie Mick and the plan was that the three of us were going to move into a flat. Days before the removal van was due to pull up outside, Mick dropped the devastating news that he was returning to Oz, leaving me and Ant to move in with each other. He was a nice bloke, a kind of English version of Mick, constantly stoned, and with a monster munch habit; but, unlike Mick, he looked like Brad Pitt. Amazing how many of my female friends at the time used to 'pop' in for a coffee. To say Ant was a bit lazy was like saying Piers Morgan can be a tad annoying. So when I broke my foot playing football, Ant did what any other friend would do in the circumstance. After I had just about made it into the lounge in our fourth floor flat, on my new cruches, with my right foot plastered to my knee, I fell onto the sofa, soaked in sweat and looked at Ant. He looked me up and down and his opening gambit should have been a bit of a hint as to what was coming. 'How long are you gonna be like that then?' he asked caringly, with a loving concern. 'About five weeks.' I replied. 'We are out of milk, I'll nip down the shop.' he said, like a true pal to his friend in need. He came back, five weeks later.

He lived by the moto: A friend in need is a pain in the arse; and moved back into his Mum's house.

So, back to the tour. Now as you may have gathered from earlier chapters, nothing was ever quite as it seemed in Smiley world. This time though, what was not to like? An arena tour, in a band with two drummers. Like the Glitter Band, or Adam and the Ants, I thought. Or me and Simon at the Royal Holloway college on our second date.

On that Thursday morning, me, and my disguised hairline fracture, turned up at Terminal Studios in London, just next to where The Shard would later dominate the London skyline. (I practically watched The Shard being built years later whilst in Archive rehearsals across a three-year period, but that's later in the book, if you still haven't found a better way of getting to sleep at night). I proceeded into studio three where I saw Richard. Gary Numan and, now, JPAC drummer. We exchanged a double drummer hug, like the Glitter and Ants lads probably had all those years before, and we waited. There was a noticeable lack of drums in the room. Two to be precise. A snare drum on each side of the stage, with a keyboard in the middle and strangely one of those sack trolleys, you know, the stand up ones with 2 handles you tip back with 8 bags of cement piled up on them at B&Q. mmm? How odd.

Then the door opened and in walked two mini East 17 lookalikes and a camp dance teacher. The two boys in the band, both smoking joints and wearing shades indoors, and a Christopher Dean lookalike in pink suede shoes rather than ice skates. Pleasantries were exchanged, and then it was down to the nitty gritty. It was instantly apparent that Rich and I were not there for our paradiddle techniques. Or our boyish good looks (Richard more than me, according to every single woman I knew). Bit of a heart throb Rich, but when I tell you the basic premise, you'll realise that those cheekbones were on the same 'not needed' list as the paradiddles. You see JPAC were like a younger, streetwise, edgier, version of The Pet Shop Boys. Bloke behind keyboard using one finger to trigger sixty-four tracks of dance music with a singer who was a cross between Olly Murs and Johnny Rotten.

Ironically, I met, CLANG! … OLLY MURS, years later in the same rehearsal studio. I told him I knew his drummer and then quickly realised he didn't know his own drummers name. Then asked him for an autograph for my daughter. He pulled out a huge wedge of pre-signed Olly Murs pics and asked me how many I wanted. Just the one thanks.

Anyway, back to JPAC and it's all getting a little bit elf costume like. You see there was more than just playing those two snare drums. Oh Yes. There was a sequenced routine involved. Steps, movement, pauses and gesturing. Add to this pushing the singer who was strapped to the sack trolley in a mask and straight jacket, while we were both dressed as surgeons with full gown, mask, and surgeon's hats. Wheeling the crazed Hannibal Lecter character into the middle of the stage, proceeding to undo his straight jacket to free the whirling snarling lunatic, as we foxtrotted our way to our waiting snares and, basically, impersonated drumming Andrew Ridgeleys while he sang 'Nutter, he's a nutter, everybody thinks he's a nutter', in a cockney accent. I shit you not. Yep. I was about to play to 7000 people a night in the biggest arenas in Europe, including Wembley, dressed as Dr Hilary Jones, and of course I had told the world and his wife of the impending shows with Brian and the guys. Deja vu anyone? Anyway, five hours later the three-song routine was ready, and the following day we set off in a very posh splitter bus with the Punk Pet Shop Boys, to support the second biggest boy band in the land.

The size of the show was incredible. East 17 had a full live band, lights, pyrotechnics, abseilers and eight dancers. It was immense. Their show would start with the four lads; Brian, the cheeky little scamp, who would later famously run himself over; Tony, the one who had written all the songs, taken all the publishing money, and was considerably richer than anyone else near the tour; John, a former roofer and; Terry, a plumber, still plumbing when not 17'ing at the weekends, and fresh off a job installing a new toilet at their management offices. All geezers. All with a proper cockney swagger, and with a show that was genuinely jaw dropping. They would be lifted up in harnesses at the start of their show and then abseil down a waterfall, dance and rap through an hour-and-twenty-minute set of more memorable hits than you would think. Stunning. (They were competing with Take That in a Blur v Oasis style boyband stand off at the time).

This is where it gets quite interesting because, also on the bill were two other opening acts. After JPAC was the new Australian singing dancing bag of bulging muscles, six packs, and curtain hair style, who sang about a mysterious girl; and, of course, you all know him by his name, CLANG! ... PETER ANDRE. Pete, as I would come to know him by, was a very nice man. Polite, courteous, always with a smile and a good morning. Always working out; press ups, sit ups, and ALWAYS looking in the mirror, because Pete loved Pete. He and his 2 beefcake dancers would sway into the dressing room area like a floating 18 pack. Huge puffa jackets and Timberland boots, and would go on stage wearing next to nothing but a bucket load of biceps, triceps, and those funny little microphones drunk girls in pubs pretend to have using straws and singing along to S Club 7. The women in the arenas went absolutely bonkers for Pete. Everyone adored him, apart from everyone on the tour. He was affectionately known as 'A bit of a knob', but the women loved him.

Also on the tour were the pop group Deuce. A piss poor, Abba like, two boy two girl outfit, who are now probably best known because one of Ant and Dec was married to, and then divorced from, Lisa, the dark haired one. They were nice enough. It's hard getting musical respect from your peers when you're dressed as an extra from Casualty whilst wheeling Hannibal Lector Jr around on a creaky unpredictable trolley, and can I point out now that a straight jacket is not easy to unstrap in front of 7000 people still trying to find their seat number in a darkened arena.

We were on first every night, and the first night was what you could describe as not quite going to plan, or, a massive cock up, as we couldn't get the sack barrow over a protruding pile of wires and ended up nearly launching Hannibal Jr into the front row. Then came the straight jacket from hell routine of not quite undoing the straps, like a formula one pit stop and Lewis Hamilton driving off with only 3 new wheels. It was horrendous, and Rich and I were given a stern bollocking and told to up our game. At least Pete was there to give me a reassuring hug, while looking in the mirror.

As the tour started to gain momentum, so did our act. We were slick, like the lovely Debbie Mcgee passing Paul Daniels a top hat with a rabbit in it, whilst still keeping her smile and eye-contact combo with the audience. Showbiz gold. As we were all getting on so well it was time to play some pranks. We were put into a huge hall backstage area in Nottingham, the hall separated by a series of moveable screens down the middle. On the left, JPAC, on the right, Peter Andre. By the time Peter and the testosterone brothers arrived, they were shown to their dressing room, now over in the far corner. Four screens making a 6ft by 6ft makeshift dressing room with the words Peter and Andre on the outside, now being occupied by three singing dancers looking like Spongebob Squarepants. They stayed in that tiny dressing room all night. We never told them. The only thing they did was squeeze a mirror in there.

East 17 were amazing onstage, a truly brilliant show. One night we were invited to a bit of a party in one of their suites. It was on the thirty-third floor. Tony liked to sit on the ledge, and liked people to join him for a chat and a beer, thirt- three floors up. I was dutifully shown to the ledge for a heineken and managed to have a twenty-minute conversation whilst gripping hold of the window ledge fearing for my life. He had no fear of heights old Tony. I, on the other hand, was now wearing dark beige pants.

CLANG! ... BRIAN HARVEY. I started hanging out out with Brian. That sounds a bit wanky I know, but I did. I don't know why. I was just your average drumming surgeon, wheeling a cannibal around on a sack barrow, but he seemed to like me. He was a fascinating character. He was really famous at this point, so he had his own security guard. He used to wind people up in bars and when they finally snapped and went for him 6ft 7 Mervyn would step in and finish the job. As I said, we were travelling in a splitter bus and East 17 were in a huge tour bus. I'd never seen one let alone been on one. In later years I would spend as much time on one as I would sharing a bed with my lovely wife. One time, Brian gave me a cheeky cockney guided tour. Upstairs in the back lounge, there was a full working studio for Tony to keep cracking out the hits. He was working on a Christmas song. I told him it was sounding good. He said he was happy with it but was looking for a title. I said I would love to stick around and help, but time was against me so, unfortunately, I couldn't 'Stay Now'. Coincidence? Who knows.

The next day was a long drive to Europe. What would you do if you were just getting into a splitter bus smelling like the inside of a fake leg, full of empty monster munch packets and overflowing ashtrays, with your band, when you hear a chirpy little geezers voice shouting from the big shiny tour bus, 'Oi Smiles, come on our bus.' I was torn. Ha ha, yeah right, for about a millisecond. Off I trotted for a fascinating journey with a hit maker, a plumber, a roofer and a little fella with a huge security guard. Did JPAC care? Well, when the East 17 tour was finished they scaled down to one surgeon, I mean drummer, and his name was Richard. I'm over it.

We toured all the major cities in Europe. It was so eye opening and exciting. The show was amazing and everyone was lovely. Especially my new pal Peter, who, in between press ups, was a genuinely nice man. Two moments then popped up that made me realise I was still quite young, immature and inexperienced. There was a wardrobe lady on the tour. She was lovely and used to give everybody vitamins. I used to pop in for a chat and one day she shut the door and asked if I would help her with something. Being the gentleman that I still am, I kindly obliged. She pulled out a table tennis bat and asked me to hit her on the backside. I laughed at her funny joke. She wasn't joking. So as people were walking to and from catering, all they could see through the wardrobe window was a lady in her mid-forties bent over a flight case, being whacked on the arse by an extremely embarrassed off duty surgeon. When I had finished, (she definitely had), she smiled and said the immortal words 'Can you send your mate Richard in?' Maybe she had a thing about uniforms, or table tennis. The other realisation that I was still a little raw around the edges was when we were at the bar in a hotel and in walked eight page three models who were staying in the same hotel and were a little bit impressed by our AAA passes that we were inexplicably still wearing on a day off. (That's another red card in touring world). They were with Brian's huge bodyguard and after a bit of a chat they invited me and Rich out for a night we would never forget. I've never forgotten that Rich and I thanked them for their kind offer but had decided on an early night as were had surgeon duties the following day. I think the word you're looking for is 'Professionals'.

The last show was in Munich in a huge arena. I had been spending a lot of time watching the E17 band in soundcheck's and at the shows. I was fascinated. The drummer was Bobby Clarke. He was awesome. A bit of loose cannon but a hell of a drummer. I watched him like a hawk. So, at the soundcheck for the final show I took up my usual position at stage left and waited for the, now regimented, House Of Love run through. No Bobby Clarke in the house. You know that dream we have all had as kids when you're at the footy and the announcer says to the crowd 'Is there anybody here who can play right wing' and 90 minutes later you're being carried off the pitch shoulder high after scoring a hat trick in the Cup final. No? Just me then (an analogy I'll use again later, but with good reason). Well this was about to become a reality. Not the hat trick bit as we weren't at the football. The bit where the musical director looked over at me and asked me to sit in on drums as Bobby was nowhere to be seen. I moved gingerly behind the 9-piece, Pearl BLX, kit, complete with triggers and pads, and for the first of many times in years to come, put in ear monitors into my star struck ears. I looked up to see 4 singers, 8 dancers, and a full band, looking straight at me. 'Two bar count into House Of Love, OK?'. 'OK' I said and after missing the first beat settled into the groove with the band. I looked around as the dancers moved in and out of synch with the lights and pyres, hundreds of lights flashing as the 4 lads sang whilst doing their best Mickey Flanagan Cockney walkabout routine. It was without doubt the highlight of my first 28 years on earth. THIS was what I wanted to do forever. I went home on an incredible high. My new best friends were Brian and Peter, neither of who I never heard from again. The lads from JPAC, who I also never heard from again. Peter Andre's brother Chris, who I did hear from again, because I had accidentally picked up his pass and he wanted it back.

I went home and shared my experiences with my nearest and dearest. And my Dad gave me some wonderful words of Dad wisdom. 'It's time to strap yourself into the musical rollercoaster son. It will go up and it will go down, but, as long as you're safely strapped in, you'll stay on' Wise words Pops.

# CHAPTER 8
## ... CHESNEY HAWKES' DOG

I was still spending good quality time with the guys from the blue cornered Spinout. The two Garys had become my good friends, and I was spending more and more time with Zak too. The Nuttall of the Garys, and Zak, were now in a very cool original London band called Face. They were being tipped for greatness. They were recording with, CLANG! ... JOHN ENTWHISTLE, legendary bass player with The Who, and they were on the verge of a big record deal. The next big thing as it were. It was great seeing Zak drumming again, as he was playing guitar in Spinout. He is as good a guitarist as he is a drummer, and he's now the highest paid drummer in the world playing with The Who, so it shows you how good he is on a six string. It was slightly surreal being around him. He was the son of the most famous drummer ever in the most famous band ever. That famous! and believe me everybody knew him.

I had a row one time with, CLANG! ... NOEL GALLAGHER, revolving around Zak. I'll tell you that story later. Anyway, one afternoon I was sat in his kitchen, Zak's not Noel's, and he was looking anxious. I asked him why, and he told me he was waiting for a phone call that could change his life forever. 'Is it The Who asking you to join?' I said, for absolutely no reason. He glared at me and said if it all went wrong it was my fault for jinxing it. God only knows why I said it. But after three rings and a lot of 'Yes, yes, ok, ok's', Zak's future as the highest paid drummer in the world, and my new name as Nostradamus Smiley, were both assured. Now I didn't put two and two together at this point. I was just chuffed for him, and a little envious obviously; but he now being a Who man meant he couldn't be a Face man, but I could. I duly got a call from the bands management and suddenly I was a Face.

So, let me, as promised, tell you the Noel story. It must have been around the year 2000, and I was at Shepherds Bush Empire watching The Who, with Zak Starkey on drums. Also there, sitting three seats away to me on my left and mainly air drumming, was Oasis guitarist and brother of Liam, Noel Gallagher. After the show I was in the backstage bar, chatting to my friend Matt Hay who was then working for the band. Behind me was Noel and about eight of his mates. As we turned face to face, I complimented him on his air drumming skills. He laughed, and I noticed he may have been a teeny-weeny bit hammered, as were all his entourage. 'He's a bit good isn't he' I said referring to the son of the Beatle and, as he agreed, Paul Stacey, a now world famous producer/guitarist, who I had by this point worked with on a few occasions, flew into the conversation. He was a big mate of Noel's. 'Alright Smiles?' he said with a hug. He then explained to Liam's brother that he hadn't seen me since we played together with Robbie. 'Williams?' said Noel. 'Yes' I replied'. 'Well then I don't wanna talk to you', and he proceeded to turn his back on me, much to the amusement of his little man gang. I tapped him on the shoulder and told him there was no reason for that. He once again announced, to his now guffawing hangers on, that he would no longer be talking to me. This went back and forth three or four times until I brazenly said, 'Why don't you ask me who I drum for now?' Silence. 'Who?', he asked, somewhat ironically, given to where we were in this conversation. CLANG! ... 'JOE STRUMMER. Is that cool enough for you Noel?'

I stuck out my chest, walked away, and didn't look back in anger.

I have a sneaky feeling that story may have gathered some legs over its copious retells through the last two decades, but the basis of it is true. To give him his dues, I met Noel again while playing with Strummer at V2000. He was side of stage with CLANG! ... PAUL WELLER, and was sharing his latest gag, with everyone within a fifty yard side of stage radius, about me being, wait for it, drumroll, Joe's Drummer. Hilarious. Then he had a drunken wee up the side of Tony Mullins's white transit. Now that joke popped up again recently with the drummer from Shed Seven trying to claim it. I duly popped him back in his place via Facebook messenger.

I've probably given away a bit about the next couple of chapters, but as I said at the start of the book this isn't going to run in perfect symmetry. And most of you know that Robbie and Strummer are on their way by association. Or by reading their names in the chapters section. It's not like I'm telling you the boat hits an iceberg and sinks, or that Milli Vanilli didn't sing on their records. In fact, to balance things up here's a CLANG! ... LIAM GALLAGHER story to balance all things Oasis up.

One day I was in Matrix studios in Chelsea, sadly no longer there but, in its day, one of the best. Situated right nearby to the footballing mecca that is Stamford Bridge. I was with Robbie, recording B sides to his third solo single Lazy Days. I had finished the fourth drum track of a very productive afternoon and Robbie had said his goodbyes and left the building, just like Elvis, but without the jumpsuit. I decided it was time for a snack and proceeded to the studio cafe where I came face to face with Liam Gallagher. THE LIAM. The 1997, swaggering, sunglasses, smoking, beer swigging, and more swaggering, Liam. 'Alright?' he said, as only he or Kathy Burke could. 'I'm Liam'. I introduced myself and he invited me to sit with him, at an empty table in the empty cafe. I asked him general, day to day, biggest rock star on the planet, questions; the best one being, 'What are you doing here today?' His genius reply? 'FOOK ALL. I'm just here to annoy my brother.'

It turns out Noel was in the next studio, with the rest of Oasis, recording The Masterplan. He then asked me my purpose of being in the, now not so empty, studio cafe. 'I'm here recording with Robbie' I replied. This must have been between the love and hate period in the Williams/Gallagher soap opera as Liam expressed his desire to hear a track. I asked him to give me a minute and went back into studio B to relay the request to Guy Chambers and Steve Power, and two minutes later the Red Stripe swigging, Benson and Hedges puffing, parka and Ray-Bans wearing, Mancunian legend, had been led in, by me, sure, and was nodding along to the loudest playback of a song I had, and have ever since, heard. After the final fade out he used the words 'Top, mega, man; sweet,' and, 'nice one'. He then shook every hand on offer, and departed, sauntering out of the room like he was walking on stage at the Brits to collect his lifetime achievement to coolness award. Quite an entrance and quite an exit. There's another part to this story so if you stick around you'll read it in about eight pages time.

Anyway, back to Face. If you speak to any musician who has been in an original band, they will tell you the two most frustrating aspects are management companies, and record companies. You are promised, reassured, confirmed, unconfirmed, and basically lied to, on a daily, sometimes hourly, basis. We were signed to both, and both were as bullshitty as the other. It was like being a liberal democrat with a fibbing tory on one side and a devious labour back bencher on the other. We played shows in London which were great; we recorded tracks which were great. We were told about single releases, album releases, tour supports, TV appearances, radio appearances and press interviews. But they never actually happened. We would shlep all the way up to the fancy big offices overlooking Regents Park Zoo, and sit in meeting after meeting, where they would be telling us of all the brilliant things we wouldn't be doing. It was frustrating to say the least.

Then another SLIDING DOOR MOMENT. I was good friends with CLANG! ... CHESNEY HAWKES. He had been The One And Only for a while but was still just Uncle Len and Auntie Carol's son to me. A really beautiful human being, who I still keep close as a friend to this day. Anyway, one day Ches asked me if I would look after his dog Poppy for a weekend while he was out of the country. I thought it sounded like a poochy idea and I gladly took delivery of the pup a day later. She was lovely.

I had only had one experience of owning a dog up until this point in my twenty-eight years. A Labrador pup I had bought a year earlier while I was living with a couple of girl friends. Ozzie was beautiful. But rather territorial. This basically manifested itself in him being loving and sweet, and super house trained, while I was there, and then turning into a naughty little bugger when I wasn't. The sign would be when I got in late from a gig. If he was in the kitchen, locked behind the baby gate, and usually with half a Breville sandwich maker hanging out of one side of his mouth, then he'd been in naughty little bugger mode. He would sheepishly come snug in with his Daddy and tell me with his puppy eyes that he hadn't meant to bite Ali and eat both her shoes. It was just a little puppy wuppy accident. We would snug in and all would be sweetness and light until I went out again the following night, and he, basically, swallowed a dustpan and brush, before proceeding to regurgitate it liberally throughout the rented house. The clock was ticking and after several months of such nightly occurrences it was agreed, two to one, that Ozzie would have to be rehomed. The next day the plans were secured and after driving him to his new loving family home, I cried. For the first time I could ever remember. Real water surging from my eyes like a shaken diet Pepsi can and a sound like a scene from Star Wars involving Chewbacca.

Anyway, back to Ches's pup. It was nice to be spending quality time with a canine who didn't have a Breville habit. And as we were walking, down by the river, that afternoon, I received a call from my new agent. Would I go and play drums for two guys in London for four hours, as their drummer had let them down and they were in pre-production for an upcoming album. No money, no expenses. Now, it's a tricky combo, money and music. Saying no to something because it isn't financially viable can be a brave call as it's sometimes those sliding door moments that turn out to be the most profitable, but there is also a fine line between taking a chance and being used and taken advantage of. I asked the question that would seal my decision. 'Can I take Chesney Hawkes' dog with me?' The next day, Poppy and I were in an East London rehearsal room with

Steve Mckewen and Fil Eisler. Both superb musicians, and both slightly curious as to why I was with the one and only's pup. Anyway, after helping the boys with their pre-production, of what were superb tunes, and some serious jamming between the three of us, we finished the session and, just as we were bringing the day to a close, I asked a question. 'So, who are you chaps writing and recording with at the moment?' They replied with ...

.. CLANG! ... ROBBIE WILLIAMS.

'Top of the Pops' in my pyjamas! 1972

Early writing session
with my Dad. 1970

Busking in Kingston with Mark and
Trevor. We made £3.50! 1986

My first gig, aged 14,
with my Dad. The
start of playing
behind my heroes.
1981

The view from the back! 2016

You Bet 1995.
Rocking the
'soft furnishings
waistcoat' look!

Wembley Arena 1996. Not quite how
I'd envisaged it.

Abbey Road 2014.
Channelling my inner Paul
McCartney ...

... probably sounding more like Bobby Crush!

Australia … with hair! 1990

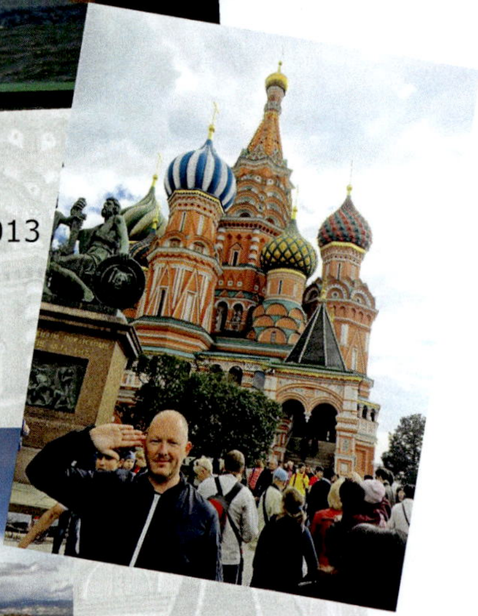

Moscow … without hair! 2013

The Grand Canyon … with a hat! 2019

'Can you sign my leg? I'll get it tattooed!' 2017

When I showed my Mum this pic, she asked if the leg was mine!

Peter Andre 1996. Not mysterious, and not a girl!

Brian Harvey. Wembley Arena 1996.

The Mock Turtles.

Manchester 2001

Four Good Men. San Francisco 2006.

Los Mondo Bongo. Liverpool 2009.

The best voices in the business!

John James Newman, Dorie Jackson, and Kerry Barnard Schultz

Cardiff 2016

Alan Thompson. 1963—2017. The original CLANG!

## CHAPTER 9
## ... AUDITION. ROBBIE STYLEE

The phone rings. It's my agent. 'Darling, how frightfully exquisite to hear from you. How the devil are you?' It didn't actually go like that but, if this book gets made into a film, Al Pacino is definitely playing my agent. I'm, however, still undecided if I will be played by Jason Statham, Bruce Willis, or Max Branning from Eastenders. Anyway, the phone call. Agent; 'Got you an audition for tomorrow in London. It's for', CLANG! ... 'ROBBIE WILLIAMS.' Amazing, I loved Robbie. 'How many drummers are going for it?' I asked, just out of curiosity. 'Twenty-six'. 'Ok, and what number am I?' 'Twenty six.'

At this time, Robbie had left Take That and had gone on a bit of a mid-life crisis mission, early. He was one of that rare breed; men wanted to be him, and women wanted to sleep with him. Everybody loved Robbie. Even in Take That. Now he was at Glastonbury, in his red adidas tracksuit top, hanging out with Oasis, blacking out his front teeth, bleaching his hair, and just having it very very large. He had just finished a week presenting The Big Breakfast. It was comedy genius. Not only was he totally infectious on screen at six thirty till nine that Monday to Friday, but he didn't go to bed, at all, so by Thursday it had turned into TV Gold. He told me once that he genuinely couldn't remember past Wednesday night. He was now a solo artist. He had done a version of George Michael's Freedom, but was now looking for a rockier edge and had a new single coming out, called 'Old Before I Die'. It was a cracker. It had swagger, a bit of Gallagher brother about it, and was all over the radio.

My audition slot was three-thirty. The last of the twenty-six. The band probably bored shitless by then, and having decided drummer number five was their man, begrudgingly going through the motions till tea-time. So, me and the Uno drove up to Kings Cross, leaving plenty of time for traffic. There wasn't any so I was bit early. I reported to reception and was given a Sony Walkman with headphones. It was 1997 (Chelsea 1 Middlesborough 0). A good omen surely. I was sent off to the cafe to learn the four songs on the Walkman. As I entered, I witnessed three drummers, frantically scoring out page after page of drum scribble.

Now I have never been a 'reader'. My drum teacher in my teens was a lovely man called John Tayler. His teaching studio was underneath the drum shop 'Footes', just off Leicester Square. My Mum and Dad would take me on the train on a Saturday morning once a month. Mr T was a formidable jazz drummer and wore brown hush puppies. For three or four years he would teach me how to play jazz, swing, groove, and, allegedly, how to 'read'. He would put the sheet music in front of me and I would play along to a record. One day we were doing Day Tripper by The Beatles. I was flying through it in true Ringo fashion but then, halfway through the second chorus, Mr T simply closed the page. He turned John, Paul and George off and looked me in the eye. 'In all my years of teaching' he said 'You are the second most natural drummer I have taught, and the second worst reader.' My future days in the West End were no more. A future of evenings spent in the pit of The Lion King were not to be. Bothered? Nope. It was never my calling. Although I have to say I have so much admiration for those West End guys.

So, back in the café; and, as the other drummers sitting with headphones on were frantically scribbling crotchets and semiquavers, I listened to the 4 tracks. They were ace. I wrote notes on the back of my left hand. Fast, slow, fast, slow. Then at half past three, as I sat all alone in the now empty cafe, a face poked around the door to lead me into studio two.

Now, this was definitely a SLIDING DOORS MOMENT. Because standing in the middle of the room, surrounded by eager looking musicians, was Robbie. He had only just arrived. The band had been putting the other twenty-five through their paces without him. Now he was actually here, and ready to perform his new songs. The band's tails were up, and all were ready to cement their positions in his new band. I then felt an arm around my shoulder. 'I wondered when you were getting here.' It was Fil Eisler from the week before's Chesney dog session. I shook hands with everyone in the room, then the man himself. He was taller than I thought he would be. He was wearing a jacket that was worth more than my Fiat Uno, and he was ready to rock. We had a hug and I sat behind the kit.

'Let's do Teenage Millionaire' said Rob. Brilliant I thought. Which one was that? Fast? Or, slow? Or, fast? Or, slow? 'Number three.' said the, impeccably groomed, Musical Director, Guy Chambers, and, after a Nirvana like guitar intro, BOOOOOM, we burst into a full on indie smash and grab tune, with Robbie in full flow like he had been set free of all his boy band schackles. Four minutes later everyone was smiling and nodding. We never did the other fast and two slows. In that four minutes I had done what none of the other twenty-five had done and ripped the roof off

... with a little help from the singer from Stoke-on-Trent.

I was asked if I would come back the next day for the guitar auditions. After checking my social engagements calendar for the following day, I happily accepted the offer. This is where it all gets a bit surreal. I said my goodbyes to everyone in the room. It was hugs all round now. And I walked off down the long, concrete, prison like, corridor. Then I heard a voice from behind me. 'Smiles, are you driving?' It was the voice of Robert Peter Williams. 'Any chance of a lift home?' Five minutes later, me and the most famous ex-boyband singer in the UK were pootling down the street in a white Fiat Uno. I said it was surreal. We chatted like old friends. We talked about football, childhood, and music. We stopped off to buy cigarettes. We chatted some more, but then, as I pulled up at some lights, the car behind didn't see my brake lights, which were probably broken anyway, and slammed into the back of us. It was more of a nudge, but I had a precious cargo, so it sounded to me like a slam. The slammer got out of his car and put his head through the passenger window. 'Sorry about that mate, didn't see you braking. Theres no real damage; if you want to just leave it and avoid insurance and, f**k me, you're Robbie Williams!' Yep, that's how the conversation went, word for word. So, after an hour's drive through the London evening traffic, I dropped my new pal off at his flat.

Day two. Guitar auditions. I walked into the rehearsal room, bright and breezy, and ready to take my position in my new band. Tea was consumed. Conversation light and easy and ready for the barrage of guitarists. The first five were awful. One even brought his own stool. The next five were really awful, with one exception. I was stunned at the lack of guitar hero.

Lunchtime; where I sat opposite, the still impeccably groomed, Guy Chambers, (in the same spot I had written fast slow fast slow on my hand twenty one hours earlier,) and I saw the look of disappointment on his face. 'I know a great guitar player who would be perfect for this' I said. He handed me his phone. A minute later a phone was ringing in Englefield Green in Surrey. 'Hi, this is Gary, sorry I can't take your call, please leave a message'. Beeeep. 'Mr Nuttall, its Mr Smiley. If you get your arse down to The Depot in Kings Cross in the next three hours you will walk into the Robbie Williams job.' Three hours later, Gary Nuttall had the Robbie job. He later told me that he had been in bed when I had called, had listened to the message and gone back to bed. Luckily though, he thought better of it, and grabbed his opportunity with both magical hands, and twenty-two years later is still Robbie's right hand man. Couldn't have happened to a nicer man.

It got around to four o'clock. My mate Gaz was in. I'm just preparing to leave, when I hear the name Michael Lee. 'He's the drummer with Jimmy Page and Robert Plant.' I thought to myself. Must be another Michael Lee. It wasn't. In walked the current hottest drummer in the UK. All long hair and leather trouser. He was a day late, for HIS audition. I gulped. I had assumed the job was mine. I offered to leave but was urged to stay and observe. The next fifteen minutes consisted of Michael Lee smashing his way through fast slow fast slow, as well as breaking a snare drum and 2 cymbals. It was brutal. 'So, when do we tour?' he said, whilst his manager placed a towel around his shoulders, like he had just gone ten rounds with

Lennox Lewis. 'We'll be in touch' said Guy. He left. They all looked at me. 'It'll cost you a fortune in cymbals' I remarked. There was a pause, then some hearty laughter. I was in, and I was strapped in, as the roller coaster was about to go up, very high.

## CHAPTER 10
## ... OLD BEFORE I DIE

My first day as Robbie's new drummer was a rather poignant one. The new album 'Life Thru A Lens' was nearly finished, and Gary and I were invited back into Maison Rouge studios in London to have a listen. After listening through what I still think is Rob's best album, Guy Chambers asked if we would sing backing vocals on the track 'One Of God's Better People'. The reason I say it is poignant is that I got given a gold disc for that album, and that backing vocal, which I gave to my Mum and Dad. It hangs in their hallway to this day.

The following day was another Smiley TV moment. Not quite You Bet, not quite Elf outfit, but bloody close. I reckon I swerved the bullet a bit, as there were five 'Prince Regent' suits hanging in the dressing room at Channel 4's TFI Friday studio's, three white, and two black. You can definitely hide better in black. I may not have been seen quite as clearly as the 'whiteys', but an old pal of mine told me that, when we kicked into 'Old Before I Die, he knew it was me, and he didn't even know I had got a new job. So he says, and so I'll take it.

It was a brilliant show in its day TFI. Chris Evans interviewing a great mix of guests, and always three live bands. Do you remember the 'it's your letters' bit, where Chris would read out viewers letters? The little musical intro to it was famously done by Reef. We did a version, which didn't surface until about twenty years later. They brought back TFI for one night and I just happened to have the night off, so Kez and I settled in for the evening, for a walk down memory lane. An hour, and a bottle of wine, into the show, Chris announced, 'It's your letters', and the top 5 theme tunes. I paused, as number five was announced, and Ocean Colour Scene did their version. My mind was ticking when The Lightning Seeds did number four. 'I'm sure we did one of these Kez' I said. Now my beloved wifey is not one for being massively overimpressed with anything showbizzy I've done in my illustrious past, but, halfway through our second bottle of Chardonnay, she looked at me like a bunny that had heard something rustle in the forest. Number three came on, can't remember who, but she was primed and ready with her phone. Then, sure enough, at number two; Robbie Williams' version, with a close up of her loving hubby, with hair, smiling at her in forty-two inches of HDMI colour. She was so proud bless her, as were her army of Facebook followers, who didn't have a clue about my hairier showbiz past. TFI I salute you.

It was next on to MTV for a live performance of three tracks from the new album. Looking back, the band Rob had was incredible. Fil Eisler went on to be a successful writer and conductor for TV and film in America; Martin Slattery would end up doing the music for Peaky Blinders; Andy Wallace actually won an Oscar for music he had written; and Guy and Gary are still in Rob's band twenty-two years later.

The MTV performance was also my first encounter with a stylist. Rob had a very debonair chap, whose name escapes me now; but our first meeting doesn't. 'OH NO' were his first words to me. He shook his head, clicked his fingers and his sidekick took me by the arm to be immediately 'styled'. It was ace, being given a shirt that was worth the same as a month's mortgage payment. I quickly found these were what's known as 'loaners', and they were impossible to steal. I tried once, by innocently keeping one on under my jacket, but was hauled in the next morning. It never happened again. The single was selling well, and it was then I heard the magic 4 words. CLANG! ... TOP OF THE POPS. Yeah baby. The show every musician dreamed of appearing on.

I started dreaming at a very early age. Three or four according to my Mum and Dad. Every Friday evening at seven thirty, I would set my little drum kit up in my bedroom. The one that my loving parents had bought their little, budding, Buddy Rich. I'd completed it with plastic ice cream tubs. Then, I'd change into my little blue silky jim-jams and be ready to play along to every song. The Sweet's Ballroom Blitz, Mud's Tiger Feet. 70's glam. It was amazing. Afterwards, I'd pack my drums down again, put them at the back of my little sister's bottom bunk bed, strap her into the passenger seat next to me, and drive us off to the next gig. Ironic really, as that was what I was still doing forty years later.

So, I was now going to be on TOTP. I had grown out of my blue silky jim-jams, and there was no way I would be able to get a new pair past the stylist, so I went with the flow. I was picked up from my house in a blacked-out Mercedes, and we cruised through Staines high street on the way to Elstree, where the TOTP studio nestled right next to Albert Square. The door to the building housing the dressing rooms was used as the hospital on Eastenders, the 'Walford General' sign laying nonchalantly by the bush on the right.

As I said at the start of the book, my recollection for times, dates, faces, and places, is pretty shocking, but I do remember a couple of strange events from that first TOTP. There really aren't that many people in the audience. It's all about camera angles and although it looks rammed with eager young teenagers screaming at the top of their lungs when Janice Long introduces you, there's really no more than about forty, trying to imitate four hundred. Sorry if I'm spoiling the illusion for you. The first thing you do when you arrive, is get shunted into the studio at your allotted time for a camera rehearsal.

Now, TOTP went through various stages of miming/live performing over the years. I did it seven times, with three different acts, and it was different every time; all miming; miming with just the singer live; and, all playing live. You never quite knew what was going to be happening when you got there. A lot of people have asked me over the years how you mime drums. The answer is simple. There are white cardboard pads on the drums, and they put two cymbals on top of each other so, when you hit them, they look like normal drums and cymbals, but sound like you're sending a message out in morse code. Tap Tap. Again, sorry if I'm spoiling the illusion, but that's showbiz folks. The other tricky thing is knowing how to mime. It's actually not as easy as it looks to be cool. I curated a method where I would try to find the TV monitor in the room, so I knew when I was on screen. Then I devised a cunning method of pretending I was having a right old laugh with the bass player who was out of shot and probably not even looking in my direction. It always looked like I was having the time of my life. I told some friends of mine years later who found a load of old Youtube footage and sure enough, I would laugh like someone had told me a hilarious gag every time the camera pointed in my direction. I thought it was cool at the time. My friends have since reassured me it wasn't. Thanks Dorie.

The other thing I remember was how mind blowing it was walking past dressing rooms with the names on the doors. CLANG! ... STING. CLANG! ... FUN LOVING CRIMINALS. CLANG! ... OCEAN COLOUR SCENE. CLANG! ... STEVE CRADOCK, once asked me if we could swap shoes. CLANG! ... HUEY MORGAN, had his own bar in his dressing room and asked if we wanted to do some tequila. CLANG! ... STING, again! He sat in the room opposite us playing his guitar while occasionally looking over and smiling. It was mesmerising. When he was performing Roxanne acoustically that evening, we were queued up in the corridor ready to follow him on. He came off stage, dressed in his silver Quadrophenia zoot-suit, and cooly walked past us all, guitar in hand. I was at the back of the Williams queue. He looked at me, probably thinking 'nice shirt, bet he doesn't get to keep it', I was thinking 'Don't say something stupid'. We engaged each other in eye contact, and I said, 'You've done this before haven't you?' 'Just a couple of times son.' said the Ace Face. He smiled, I smiled. He walked off into the distance and I turned back round. 'You wanker!' the queue in front of me universally said. Fair point.

Then we were ushered to the stage in our rented shirts and waited to be introduced by a Radio One DJ who I can't remember. Forty kids, making the same noise as four hundred at a One Direction school assembly appearance, screamed on cue. Then we heard the presenter say the magic words 'ROBBIE WILLIAMS'; cue crowd noise, cue guitar intro, cue shot of drummer in expensive shirt pretending to be having a right laugh with the bass player whilst actually making the noise of a teacher writing on a black board. Oh, the power of television. Three minutes and thirty seconds later, we were walking back down the same corridor, past Westlife. That's showbiz folks.

Top of the Pops was recorded on a Thursday, and went out at seven-thirty on a Friday. Whilst I was starring on BBC1 that rainy Friday evening, I was actually stuck in a traffic jam on the A3, with Crucial Chris, en route to a pub gig in Kingston (keeping it real). I sat in the passenger seat, looking at all the houses, and hoping they would be tuned into BBC1, noting what a right laugh Robbie's drummer was having, and how nice his shirt was. I waited for my phone to ring. It didn't. I realised the next day that the world didn't stand still for me, or Old Before I Die on Friday night's TOTP. My Auntie Marion enjoyed it though.

The next Robbie TV experience was like a dream come true for me. The ITV Sports Awards. A room full of sports stars, and musical appearances from us, The Lightning Seeds, ironically with Zak Starkey playing drums, and, CLANG! ... LOUISE REDKNAPP. I remember walking back from our camera rehearsal and standing next to her dressing room door. She was alone inside, in a tracksuit; looking stunning, in a tracksuit. 'Hi' she said, and promptly invited me in. She made me a cup of tea, and we sat and chatted. After the normal, pre tea, conversation tactics, I moved toward the subject of football, her husband Jamie and her father-in-law Harry. 'Oh, I can't stand football,' she explained, 'It's all Jamie and his Dad ever bang on about.' Sorry Louise, but at that moment, even if you were thinking about divorcing Jamie and declaring your undying love for your new tea drinking bezzie, you'd just blown it.

We were wheeled out during the second commercial break, ready to mime. I remember, CLANG! ... ULRIKA JOHNSON, was presenting with someone else, who I don't remember at all. All I could think was, Ulrika ka ka ka! Back from the ads, a quick intro from the 'whoever he was', and Ulrika ka ka ka, and, hello Saturday night telly. Here we go again. My friends were playing in a pub that night in Overton, so I wrote, 'Hello Overton' on one drum and, 'Hello Mum' on the other. It was the least I could do.

I had noticed Robbie was in a slightly mischievous mood during our earlier backgammon sesh. He always had a cheeky boyband wink to camera look about him, but today was extra boybandy, like he had something cheeky up his sleeve. Three minutes and twenty nine seconds later I found out what his plan was; as the final chords of the song faded out, and with the cream of the British Sport community applauding, he launched himself over the drums and piled on top of me like a Welsh scrum half. I saw him coming but he's quick off the mark old Rob, and before I knew it I'd flown off the back of my drum stool and was lying flat on my back on the studio floor. For a split second I blacked out, only to come around and realise that Rob and the band had buggered off and left me there, and Ulrika ka ka ka was now halfway through introducing the award for Best British tracksuit wearer. I picked myself up and sheepishly attempted to discreetly smuggle myself off stage, whilst being laughed at by, CLANG! ... PHIL TUFFNELL, who was sitting next to,

CLANG! ... RON ATKINSON. There's one to tell my grandchildren. Cos hopefully I'll be old before I die.

# CHAPTER 11
## ... LAZY DAYS

Once the Old before I die single had finally charted and flown off into the sunset, we were given around six weeks off from Robbie duties. I just did what I did before and went back to playing the pubs. Nothing had changed. I didn't get a bigger pub dressing room, there were no screaming teenagers at the bar, and there were no pap's hiding in the snug. In fact, the closest I came to a bit of fame was when I was stood behind Crucial Chris at the bar at a university. It was during the break in the gig, just after Freebird, and a guy tapped him on the shoulder. 'Are you the one who plays with Robbie?'. Bless I thought, they have the wrong member. Go on, put him straight CC. 'That's me' he joyously replied, and then repeated three Robbie related stories that I had previously told him, got a free pint and swished back on stage with not a care in the world, and a new fame fuelled drink in his hand.

To be honest, nothing really changed after my TV appearances. I got a few 'saw you on the telly's', and my Mum would comment on my expensive looking shirts (I didn't shatter her illusions regarding the rental part); but, apart from that, it was pretty much as you were. The only awkward situation was with Face. The singer wasn't particularly happy that half his band were now in another, slightly more high profile line up. This concluded with him turning up to a Robbie rehearsal in London and stating this as being the case rather too loudly for myself and Gary to handle. The next day we were Faceless. The price of fame eh.

Soon it was back to promo for the next Robbie single 'Lazy Days'. Rob was being managed by two fabulous gentlemen by the names of Tim Clark and David Enthoven. They were the perfect ying and yang management combo. David, larger than life itself, and fabulously loud with a constant grin on his face, an immediate piss-take with every greeting, usually about my now thinning thatch. A beast of a man in every sense of the word whose life was like a feature film, with him being played by Marlon Brando in his pomp. Tim, on the other hand, was cool, calm, and extremely laid back. Always friendly and receptive, and never took the piss. Ladies and gentlemen the perfect management double act to steer the now footloose and fancy-free ex-boyband heartthrob on the right course.

I realised quite quickly, however, that the course setting could take some time. You see Rob was now in rehab. None of us had seen or heard from him since the sports awards show, but we were tipped off about the current situation as we arrived at the Top of the Pops studios to record our Lazy Days performance. We ran the camera rehearsals without him. After a happy run through for all the lights and camera angles we went to the canteen. This was shared with the cast of Eastenders, and one of the best moments of my adult life occurred as I turned left at the till and literally bumped into, CLANG! ... BARBARA WINDSOR. Yes! BABS WINDSOR. The woman who, nearly single handedly, had steered me through puberty, with the assistance of all three Charlie's Angels, Daisy Duke and Wonder Woman. I immediately turned into a cross between Sid James and Bernard Bresslaw as I made my apologies. Incredibly, she gave me one of her famous little Carry On giggles and said, 'Thats alright my darling.' It was the most surreal moment of my adult life up to that point and, as the world stopped spinning, and I had visions of Babs, first surrounded by tents, in a skimpy yellow bikini, then immediately followed by a blue and white nurses uniform. I uttered my usual nervous retort. 'Aren't you lovely.' This obviously could have, possibly, ended one of two ways. With a Sting like 'wanker' from everyone in the canteen, or a slap round the choppers from a living British institution. Surprisingly, it was neither of the above, and, in a moment I will genuinely never forget, she said 'So are you.' With that, she giggled, and we had a little cuddle. It was a moment I will never forget. I'm amazed her bra stayed on really.

After a moment of readjustment, I pulled myself together, set my tray to a North Westerly direction and headed for the lasagne. 'Hiya Smiles.' said a rather gaunt looking chap with a shaved head. I did a double take. It was Robbie, fresh out of rehab and looking like a completely different person. He must have lost two stone in weight as well as most of his lush thick hair. Jealous? Me? Nooo. We both smiled and then we had a hug. The second-best hug that lunchtime. Did I mention that, CLANG! ... MARTINE McCUTCHEON, had been standing next to Babs, and that, CLANG! ... PHIL MITCHELL, (Steve McFadden), was eating spaghetti right in front of me. No? No reason. We all finished our delicious pasta dishes and went back to our dressing room.

If I recall rightly, we were next to Westlife, or Boyzone, or Blue. I genuinely can't remember as they all looked and sounded the same to me. Rob and I sat and played a bit of backgammon and, before we knew it, we were constructing a curious plan of action. My day couldn't get any more surreal, could it? We were going to break into Albert Square. Why? Because it was Albert Square and it was just over there. Me, Rob, Fil and Ricky, Rob's security bloke, decided we were going to see just how far we could get into the square. We discussed last minute plans and set off towards Walford. We found the fence adjacent to the Queen Vic and saw the square was clear as they were filming down by Dot's launderette, next to Ali's cafe. This is taking you back isn't it? We jumped the fence and made it to the hedge surrounding the square. The bit where the shot of a black cab pulling away is always used, accompanied by sad music, whenever someone is leaving the show, probably to try and crack Hollywood, but inevitably to end up back in the Square ten years later, with a different face. We looked at each other. A drummer, a bass player, a pop star, and a bodyguard, crouched like nine-year-old's, planning on breaking into the next-door school to nick their volleyballs. 'Now what?' one of the four said. Silence. The dare was then struck to get to the Queen Vic and, subsequently, get inside, nick a pint glass as a souvenir, and get out again, without security catching us and Rob ending up on the front page of the following day's Sun newspaper. Suffice to say, our mission was halted when a very charming man with a german shepherd casually walked around the corner and said it was time to leave. Rob had got onto an episode the year before, talking on the phone in the Queen Vic when he was there with Take That. It wasn't going to wash again, so we all mooched back, pint glassless. I should have just asked my new friend Barbara.

Back to TOTP, and we were to mime the track with Rob singing live. Now, there was a one bar gap before the outro of Lazy Days. In between Rob singing 'Stiil got'; 2 beat pause; 'TIIIMMMMEEE.' Just enough time to throw my stick up in the air, before joyously catching it, like Shane Warne at backward square leg, and triumphantly proceeding to the end of the track, and to the mass applause of about forty girls pretending to be four hundred. What if I dropped it? The whole outro of a song on BBC1 at 7.30 on a Friday played with one stick. Viewers of all ages and gender in their lounges, looking over at each other and mouthing the words 'What a plonker.' There were two options. Either, 1; a spare stick in my back pocket You Bet stylee as a back up in case Shane spills the catch. Or, 2; Don't do it. I chose option 1.

We were introduced by Cathy Dennis, as they were using celebrity guest presenters at this point; the watching public in the studio, and probably at home too, were genuinely shocked at how much weight Rob had lost, but he was ace at live TV. The perfect balance of tuning and cheeky looks to camera. I had found the TV monitor and thrown out at least two fake laughs in the direction of the bass player. We got to the break. Two beats heading towards me like Robin Hoods arrow in a Bryan Adams video. 'Everything I do, I do it for you' I thought. I didn't really. Shall I or shan't I? Hero or villain? TV star or knobhead? I thought of Jain. Youtube or You've been framed? I did it. I threw it. I dropped it. I pulled the second stick out immediately. Luckily, no one noticed, or cared, as the camera was firmly fixed on Gary's burgundy Gibson SG guitar at that particular point of the two-beat stop. I got away with it and gave myself a ruddy good dressing down in the back of the blacked-out Merc on the way back to Staines, via Gary's house, as his was first.

Lesson learnt, the next journey into telly world was a belter. Live and Kicking, BBC1, on Saturday morning with, CLANG! ... ZOE BALL, and, slightly smaller, but still deserving of a, CLANG! ... JAMIE THEAKSTON. It was brilliant. Kids everywhere. Puppets. Rugrats. Zoe bombing around on roller skates. What's not to love?

I'd met Zoe years before at a theatre in Woking. Do you remember the posh mother of the girlfriend a few chapters back? Well ironically, I was with her, and her daughter obviously. The incredibly tall and rather delicious ZB tapped me on the shoulder from row J to ask if I was the drummer with The Mock Turtles. That impressed the mother. Again, I don't know why I remember this, as I regularly forget to buy some toothpaste after being asked by Kez forty-five seconds earlier, somewhere between the dog food aisle and the yoghurts; but I remember that ZB was wearing a very blue dress. She was doing afternoon kids telly at that point, way before waking the nation with her lovely easing voice and middle of the road corporate music. You see she was good friends with all the Turtles, Mocks, not Ninjas, and I had, apparently, briefly met her at a gig. Anyway, we chatted in the interval and, somewhat bizarrely, she gave me the phone number of the man in charge of kids telly at the BBC, as she thought I would make a great kid's presenter. I could have been the next Phillip Schofield or Gaz Top. I did actually call, and eventually received one of the famous 'BBC rejection letters'. I really must find it, it's like a Blue Peter badge for losers.

Anyway, back to Zoe Ball, and back to the Live and Kicking studio. We've been ushered in at the far end to mime a Saturday morning version of Lazy Days. Zoe is on the far side, on roller skates, surrounded by children and cameras. She looked across, and in the very excitable way like she does on Strictly, started waving her hands furiously, and zooming towards us like Jayne Torville, but without the ice. Robbie gave his band his legendary cheeky chap smile and jokingly said 'Come to Robbie.' Zoe headed straight for him and as he prepared to pukka up, she glided round him, like Bradley Wiggins overtaking in the Tour de France, and wrapped her long arms around Robbie's drummer, planted a kiss on him and said 'How's my Smiley?' in front of a, slightly startled, former Take That member. I basked in that glory for ages. Trust me, I never got one over on Rob again.

It was around this time that I'd done my first recordings with the RW band. Or, Muff Sandwich, as he liked to introduce us. We were in Maison Rouge studios; remember the Liam story? And, remember I said there was another part to that story? Stay tuned, it's coming. We were recording B sides for the upcoming singles South of the border, Angels, and Let Me Entertain You. I remember an absolute belter, co written by Gary Nuttall, called 'She Makes me High'. This was the first time I met Matt Hay, the studio assistant engineer. What a wonderful and talented man he was, and still is. We remain firm friends to this day. So, the day had reached a close. We'd had the, CLANG! ... LIAM GALLAGHER, visit, recorded several excellent B sides, and were due back in the following morning at ten.

When Gary and I walked in at ten-thirty the following morning, (he was driving!!) our lateness was met by a whispering committee of Guy Chambers, Matt Hay, and co producer Steve Power. They rushed us in, closed the door and sat us down. They were like excited school children when they announced, holding up a gold CDR disc with the words 'Be Here Now' in pen written on it, that a slightly drunk, CLANG! ... NOEL GALLAGHER, had left the said disc in the canteen, late the previous day, and it was now in the hands of Muff Sandwich. So, what's the big deal about this I hear you ask? Well, the third Oasis album wasn't due out for another two months, and nobody had heard a note. It was being kept under tight security. Unless you're the pissed songwriter and guitarist, and you leave it on a chair in the studio canteen. 'Can we hear it?' I asked. They pressed play. Helicopter noises filled the room as guitars started wailing at top volume and, 'D'You Know What I Mean' burst though the speakers like a tidal wave. Meanwhile, Matt was making copies for everyone. It was immense. Three tracks later, and we all had a copy in our bag to take home. Four tracks later, and we had all been hauled into the studio manager's office, and were made to return those copies, before noon, as Noel had threatened legal action. In hindsight, we didn't miss out on much really as the bargain buckets of Woolworths and Our Price would later reveal, but at the time, Oasis were as hot as a cheese and ham toastie, in a Breville sandwich maker, in a sauna. That hot!

## CHAPTER 12
## ... SOUTH OF THE BORDER

It was time to begin rehearsals for the upcoming UK and European tours. We were based at Music Bank in Bermondsey, London. We had the posh studio at the top, with a little roof terrace. Very quaint, and bloody expensive, apparently. It was an exciting time, but a slightly strange time. Following the disappointing chart display from Lazy Days, and knowing Angels would be out in time for the Christmas market, the record company decided to put out South Of The Border as the third single, as opposed to the originally scheduled, Let Me Entertain You. I was a bit gutted at the time as LMEY was, and is, an absolute drumming dream. Chris Sharrock, my favourite drummer, had played on the album before going off to join World Party, hence me taking over, so it was a blast playing his parts. He's still my favourite drummer and is currently a High Flying Bird. Lovely chap.

So, two days into rehearsals our tour manager, Andy Franks, a tremendous man who only ever wore black and later went on to manage Coldplay, informed us of the following day's schedule; 11am rehearsal; 2pm visit to the Kangol store to rinse them of everything on their shelves; from there, on to Luton airport; private jet to Italy; police escort to a town square, where we would mime to South Of The Border in front of five thousand screaming Italians; once that was done; police escort back to airfield; private jet back to Luton; and home; by 10pm, just in time for Match Of The Day. That was the only time I went on a private jet. I can see the appeal. You can play music as you're taking off. We had Back In The USSR at full volume. It was an incredible feeling. 'This is the future' I thought. It wasn't.

The next day at rehearsals was just as surreal though. It was an incredibly hot day, and at lunchtime I popped into the loo for a quick wee. There are two studios on the top floor at Music Bank. There's always a big-name act in the other one. CLANG! ... THE SPICE GIRLS, were in the week before us, but this lunchtime, as I stood sweating up against the urinal, a beast of a man appeared on my left. No shirt, long shaggy hair, and sweating profusely. He smiled and said 'hot isnt it?' 'Sure is' I replied, to Led Zeppelin rock legend, CLANG! ... ROBERT PLANT. He was like the lion in the Wizard of Oz, but like a sex god version already loaded with courage. I've never forgotten that moment. I'm sure he says the same.

Following rehearsals, the day after that, we went to some industry do at the Shepherds Bush Empire. It was a bit of a dull affair but, suddenly, things warmed up when Rob spotted a legend. CLANG! ... ROLF HARRIS. At this point, in 1997, Rolf Harris was a global superstar. Still is, but for slighty shiftier reasons. Rob and I discussed how to approach him and what to say. It was a tricky situation and one we didn't want to mess up. After a quick rock paper scissors, I lost and got handed the job, and slowly moved forward. The bearded Australian childrens entertainer turned and looked me straight in the eye. Before he could say 'Can you guess what it is yet?' I hit him with my best shot. 'No one blows into a piece of wood like you Rolf.' Didgeridoo? More like didgeri-don't. That was the end of that conversation. Rob thought it was funny. Rolf didn't.

We decided it had now a really dull do anyway, and we headed out to go to the cinema in Notting Hill instead. We opted to see LA Confidential. It's quite a bizarre thing going to the cinema with a superstar. I got the tickets. He got the munchies. He signed 14 autographs. I didn't.

The following day was video day for the new single. This basically comprised of Muff Sandwich playing in a room at the top of a flat which was on fire and gradually through the three and half minute video we got hotter and hotter before the fire brigade broke in and we all jumped out of the window. Of course, in video world this was us in a TV studio with lots of smoke, and women continually spraying us in the face with water between takes to make us look like we were about to be burned alive. I was given a small cameo acting role which comprised solely of a close up of me slowly wiping my brow. Bafta material right there. It's on Youtube.

Those video days go on forever, you do the same run through fifteen times for different camera angles, and then the director starts going off road with whacky ideas that usually take ages to set up and are very rarely used, otherwise they would have been in the original script, right? Anyway, over lunch that day there was a discussion going on about the upcoming UK tour and the need for a warm-up show. Various ideas were being touted round and so I thought I would throw in 'The Woking Planets', where my partner at the time was events manager. I cracked on with my caesar salad with low fat dressing and sparkling water on the side, and was quietly minding my own business, rehearsing my brow and back of hand combo ready for my close up, when a member of the production team started asking me lots of questions about the Woking venue. Size, capacity, loading access etc. All the things I knew absolutely nothing about. I passed details of the venue manager across and carried on with my Bafta award winning day. The following morning, I was being treated like a hero by management, production, lighting, and everyone else in rehearsals, for sorting the Robbie Williams tour warm up show. Some pound notes in an envelope, for a finders fee, wheeled their way into the back pocket of my 501's from Rob's management. The same came from the venue/local council who were now licking their lips at the prospect of the hottest pop star in the UK lighting up the Woking skyline. If it had been Christmas, I could have probably swung him turning on the lights. My new found power as an agent was reaping its benefits.

It was around this time that I made the first of two bad moves within the Williams camp. We were on a flight to Europe. I can't remember where, when, or why, but you've already got the gist of that from the previous chapters. Anyway, Rob was to be sitting next to Guy in business class, while the rest of the band and crew were at the back. Pretty standard practise. Guy was the writer, producer and musical director; so he was totally worth his place in a bigger seat with more leg room. As we were shuffling toward the back of the plane, Rob called me from his big seat. 'Smiles, come sit with me and play backgammon. Guy won't mind.' What would you have done? Suffice to say, minutes later my legs were beautifully rested and ready for action at the other end of a most enjoyable backgammon business class type of flight. Apparently, a certain someone in cattle class wasn't quite so happy. As I said, this was the first of two bad decisions I would later come to regret.

The other took place in a hotel room in Germany; mid European tour. Rob and I were noodling around watching the footy, with a bit of backgammon thrown in, when he suddenly handed me an acoustic guitar and said, 'Lets write a tune'. Again, I ask you, what would you have done in my situation? We proceeded to play around with a few chords and melodies, Rob scribbling down lyrics while I crafted a counter melody, and, twenty minutes later, Robbie Williams's new song, 'Love Is shit' was finished, co-written with me. It was catchy and breezy, with a clever quirky lyric about love, being shit. We smiled at each other, we may have even high fived, we probably had a man hug and we would definitely have celebrated with a game of BG. Andy Franks came in. Rob insisted on debuting L.I.S to him. He threw me a slightly, 'UH OH' glance. Strange, I thought, he hasn't even heard it yet. After our performance, he gave us a generous round of applause before whispering, 'Be careful' in my ear. I was slightly baffled. Be careful how I spend my millions, now I've co written a future hit with the UK's favourite singing superstar maybe? No. It was then that Mr Chambers entered the room. Once again Rob insisted on performing the now honed and perfected future worldwide hit. Three and a half minutes later we finished our performance. There was no applause. Just the words, 'You can go now Smiley', as Guy took the guitar from my hands. Love Is shit never made the charts. It was never recorded. I never wrote with Rob again, and I never had to worry about spending my millions from its royalties.

Now, around this time was one of the strangest, and possibly saddest, day's I can recall in my lifetime. We were rehearsing at 11am. I agreed to pick Gary up at nine-thirty. As I drove the 10 minutes to his house, I couldn't understand the feeling around me. There were no cars on the roads. There was no pop music on the radio. On any of the stations. Just this somber, classical, background music, that was really eerie. I put on the news channel and realised very quickly that The Princess of Wales had been killed. That day driving to London and rehearsing was memorable but for the wrong reasons. We all know where we were that day. Angels seemed particularly powerful at that rehearsal.

Some time later, we were lucky enough to play at the Princess Diana memorial concert at Battersea Power Station. It was an emotional night, bloody freezing if I remember rightly, and I found it hard to keep warm in my nice, expensive, John Smedley shirt. My faking chilliness potential still didn't blag me a free bit of clobber. It was never gonna happen. On the bill that night, amongst others was, CLANG! ... GARY BARLOW. At that particular point, Rob and Gary weren't the best of friends, so it was quite interesting to see the dynamic between them, as by this point their solo careers were passing each other with Rob heading toward mega stardom and Gary not too far away from using the words, 'Have you been to a Harvester before, let me show you to your table'. We sat and had a band meeting discussing the best way to 'get up Gary's nose'. Various plans were hatched, some repeatable, some not, before deciding to do a version of the, Barlow written, Take That classic, 'Back For Good', but obviously with a twist. We would sing the first verse as God, and Gary, had intended. A wonderful song with touching lyrical content. What we decided to do was perform the chorus as a, full-on, Punk Rock, Sex Pistols, onslaught. It was hilarious. There is footage somewhere of GB watching it on the TV backstage, pretending to be laughing at the gag.

He wasn't. He was fuming. I'd like to take this opportunity to take full credit for that version, which Robbie would perform for years to come. Ironically, it was Rob who, inadvertently, relit the Take That fire, years later, by not turning up to a reunion to be screened on ITV. It was going to be an hour and a half look at the Take That career, with interviews with all five members; culminating in a reunion in a hotel room, which Rob decided at the last minute not to attend. The documentary exploded TT back into the stratosphere and as we all know, Robbie later rejoined the band, became friends again with Gary, and they all lived happily ever after. Remember folks, the moral of this story is; today, this could be, the greatest day of our lives. I will leave that with you as the end of this chapter, because, lets face it, we all love a happy ending.

## CHAPTER 13
## ... THE SHOW OFF MUST GO ON

It was time to hit the road. We were rehearsed and had a warm-up show under our belts, which had bought me a load of kudos with friends, as I had managed to blag fifty tickets. Amazing how many Robbie fans I knew. There were sixteen UK and fifteen European dates. The first show, and, yes, I have had to look it up, was in Norwich. In spit of my shocking memory, I can recall the routine that fell into place from the start. It went like this; after the show we would get back to the hotel, where Rob would be rushed through by security, past all the waiting fans, who somehow always knew where he was staying, and then I would follow him, with no massive need for security, up to his room where we would put music on, play backgammon, and drink water, until he was ready to sleep. I would leave him usually by about two or three'ish, and go to my room.

The first thing I would wake up to, the next morning, would be him knocking on my door wanting to do something. Usually playing football somewhere, or more backgammon (We kept the score on that tour and he beat me 401 to 399). That's a lot of BG. We played everywhere. There was one night we stayed up all night, to watch the funeral of Michael Hutchence, lead singer with INXS and former boyfriend of Kylie, who had tragically died the week before. I actually toured, years later, with a tour manager called John Martin. He told me how he was the one who opened the hotel room door to find Michael hanging on the back of it. Tragic. I always liked him and his band. I saw them at Wembley stadium back in the nineties and years later, while rehearsing in London, was lucky enough to bump into, CLANG! ... JON FARRIS. He was their drummer. I say lucky; I was actually having a wee, and he came and stood next to me. I remember he still had drumming gloves and a microphone on. I regaled my tale of my Wembley attendance and he graciously shook my hand, with drumming gloves on, straight after a wee. Memorable, but probably not the most hygienic.

Another memorable after show scenario was for all the wrong reasons. We were playing in Newcastle, and I had invited two Geordie girls from the Blue Anchor in Staines, where we used to play every Sunday lunchtime. Everyone has a favourite pub from their youth and the Anchor would be the top of a lot of lists, mainly due to Sylvia and Dave, the best landlord/lady combo in the business. Anyway, the Newcastle show was a belter and when we arrived back at the hotel there were a lot of fans waiting for the Muff Sandwich frontman. To our surprise Rob decided against our usual routine of Evian and board game, and announced to the waiting Geordie fraternity that he would happily sit around the piano in the foyer with Guy, and lead a jolly old sing along, as long as he didn't have to sign any autographs. In his words, 'If I sign one, I'll have to sign a hundred.' Fair enough, everyone thought, apart from two. The singalong was in full swing, with everyone joining in, in their Geordie accents, until one of the two rather drunken nightmares leaned across the piano and insisted on an autograph. Rob politely pointed out again that, if he signed one, he would have to sign a hundred, and so we would instead have a once in a lifetime, jolly old sing along. This simply wasn't good enough for said, hammered, visitors from Staines, and words were exchanged, drinks were thrown, pop star was grabbed by security and rushed out of the room, girls exited from the building, and sing along prematurely ended. Who would invite people like that to such a civilised get together? UH OH. The next morning on the bus, everyone was ushered into the back lounge and asked by security who had invited the two Geordie nightmares. Nobody owned up, so warnings were issued to everyone about future conduct and guest list procedure was re-examined. Lesson learnt. I'm owning up now. It never happened again. Hang on, yes it did.

Years later, when I was on tour with Archive in Switzerland, I came offstage to a phone bulging with messages referring to an altercation at a From The Jam show in, yes you've guessed it, Newcastle, involving, yes you've guessed it, a pissed up Geordie mate of mine who I had sorted tickets for, and who had ended up being thrown out for having a shouting row with the singer, mid gig, about wanting his plectrum. At the time it was a nightmare, and the FTJ camp were pointing fingers firmly in my Swiss direction. I managed to swerve the blame and get my mate Guy to take the blame. No thanks to you, Mr Nigel Adams, you, seven foot, pissed up, Geordie gobshite.

So, back to the tour, and Southampton. A very special show for me, as it was attended by my Mum and Dad, and also by my favourite Auntie and Uncle combo, Bill and Marion. They loved it. They came backstage and met Rob and the band, and were sober, polite, articulate, and very un-geordie like. Watch and learn Nige. They told me how proud they were and, as I walked off toward the tour bus, I knew that, in their eyes, I was super cool. Twenty minutes later, the bus had broken down on the M3 and, as we were all standing outside on the hard shoulder, having a wee, so my parents and favourite Auntie and Uncle combo drove past, waving, and beeping their horn. They were still so proud. Didn't bloody pull over though.

Around this time on Radio One was a DJ named, CLANG! ... CHRIS MOYLES. He would later go on to present the breakfast show and become quite a famous man. At this point though, he was presenting the graveyard shift, from two o'clock to six o'clock I the morning. We played a live session on the, CLANG! ... JO WHILEY, lunchtime show, at the, world famous, Maida Vale studios, and afterwards I got chatting to Chris, who was there watching. He was a lovely chap and he liked the fact that I knew who he was from when he was a DJ on Capital Radio. Me and my mate Si used to love listening to him on the way home from gigs. We exchanged numbers and the following day he invited me onto his ridiculously timed radio show. He thought it would be hilarious to announce having Robbie Williams whilst coughing every time he followed the announcement with the word 'Drummer'. A fine gag which would brighten any postman or milkman's round.

They sent a car for me and I arrived at 4am. I sat outside the studio, with several coffees, like I was waiting for a job interview, before finally being called in, and chatting with Chris live on Radio One about all sorts of nonsense. Ironically, through the glass in the next studio was my, by now, lovely pal, CLANG! ... ZOE BALL, getting ready for her new breakfast show. Small world showbiz. After the show, I invited Chris and his team to our London show the following night. It was a great night and, afterwards, we met in the bar for a cheeky drummer and Radio One DJ pint. CLANG! ... MARK OWEN, had been in our dressing room earlier that evening. A very nice man, smaller than you think, but extremely handsome. In the bar, Moylesy, as I now knew him, spotted Mark and told me he was due to have him as his guest on his upcoming weekend show. Having never met him he asked me to introduce them. This fame thing eh! I duly obliged.

After downing a couple more cheeky pint's, Chris spotted, CLANG! ... SAMANTHA FOX, on the other side of the room. He dared me to go say hello, and a wager was set. I approached her and introduced myself out of ear shot, and very quickly explained that the Radio One DJ over in the corner had dared me to kiss her. I asked if there was any way she could help, and she duly popped a lovely page three smacker on me and waved to Chris. Innocuous bar banter at its best. Well, a few days later I was in Rob's hotel room, doing what we did eight hundred times in eight weeks, when his phone rang. After answering it he informed me it was the tour manager looking for me. 'I'd ring home if I were you.' was his message. Dutifully, I called my then partner, who asked me what the hell was going on with Samantha Fox? It turns out Moyles had told the story about our little game of page three truth or dare, but embellished it into a 'Robbie's drummer pulled Sam Fox within twenty seconds of meeting her' story. My partner's Dad, being a milkman, had heard said story at 4am, and told his daughter. Doghouse.

Another strange story from the tour happened after our Birmingham show. I met a lovely girl; very pretty and intelligent, and with an admirable moral fibre. She told me quite fervently how women who sleep with pop stars are wrong on so many levels. An insult to the female kind. She told me that talking to me was so much more satisfying than hankering after the pop star, and that our articulate conversation was inspiring on so many levels. It was lovely to meet someone with such a refreshing moral standing. We said our goodbyes assuming we would never meet again. The following night I saw Miss Birmingham again, (she was actually Miss Birmingham) coming out of Rob's room at about 4am. Funnily enough, she wasn't quite as chatty.

It was a fantastic tour, helped by The Supernaturals, our fabulous Scottish support act. They should have been huge, and, apparently, did make a shed load of money, not from album sales but from the use of their song, 'Smile', in about twenty different cereal commercials. On one of our days off in Germany, we played against them at football. Franksy, being the greatest tour manager ever, found a pitch, and even refereed the game himself. We beat them comfortably, and my exquisite link up play with young Mr Williams was noted by management as, the next day, I was invited to play at the Soccer Six celebrity football tournament, with Rob and Mark Owen, playing for The Lightning Seeds. Never quite worked that one out, but it was played at Fulhams Craven Cottage ground, and there were thousands of Take That fans there screaming everytime Mark, Rob, and me touched the ball. Ok, Mark and Rob. They did all scream at me once, when I scored an own goal and we went out 3-2 to Shed 7 in the quarter final. Fame at last. Football. Isn't it ... Wasn't it ... Marvellous.

We were on the Rotterdam leg of the tour, when we had a night off. Rob was due to present an award at the MTV Music awards, live on the telly. He even created a special nod that he would give to the camera just for us. We all decided to stay in and watch the show. A few drinks were consumed and then out of a bag came some space cakes, which had been purchased in Amsterdam the previous evening.

For those of you who are unaware, as I was, of what a space cake consists of, it's basically a tasty muffin, but laced with cannabis. I had never smoked dope. Drugs were never my bag, and up until now I hadn't really been massively exposed to it, other than in the back of a car sitting next to Crucial Chris on the A303, looking at Stonehenge, on our way to The Monster Raving Loony conference in Devon. It was his kind of tribute to the druids. I didn't smoke it with him, but I was still stoned. Bloody hippies. Anyway, back in a hotel room in Rotterdam and the members of Muff Sandwich had devoured all the muffins which came in various flavours, mine being banana. Now the Psychodelic brain bending didn't kick in for quite a considerable time, way past the appearance of our gracious leader on the podium next to a famous hollywood actress tipping his yellow tinted glasses to his, about to be stoned band, all the way from Amsterdam. Three hours later he was back in the room which completely freaked everyone out as they were repeating the show, and he walked in at exactly the same time as he walked onto the telly. The words 'you're twisting my melon man' never seemed so relevant.

## CHAPTER 14
## ... ANGELS

Have you ever been on a first date with two of the UK's hottest pop stars? I have. We were recording out in the country. Late afternoon, Rob told me he had a date that night with that lovely Canadian All Saint sister, CLANG! ... NICOLE APPLETON. I had met her and the other Saints previously at Top of the Pops and they were all lovely. She was on her way over and, after she had arrived and pleasantries were exchanged, the three of us jumped in the vocal booth to lay down some backing vocals. You could feel the chemistry in the booth. The animal attraction between man and woman sizzling like a burning hot skillet. Sexual tension about to explode like a pre-eruption volcano. You could see it in her eyes. I think she quite liked Robbie too.

When we had finished the backing vocals and established who liked who, the two lovebirds decided to go to the local pub for their first date together. Lovely. Just the three of us. You see, I was the only one driving, and so it was left to me to be uberring the pop stars to the local, in my ageing and a bit too small for comfort Fiat Uno, with various puffa jackets squeezed in amongst us (hers was bright orange). God, I remember the strangest things. I pulled up outside the Wheatsheaf and Conker, or whatever it was called, and asked if they wanted picking up later. They insisted I joined them for a drink. I genuinely tried to get out of it but, at their insistence, ten minutes later the three of us were the only trio in a random pub, somewhere in the middle of the country. Not a Sun reporter in sight. I made my excuses after fifteen minutes, and lent him twenty quid to get a cab back to the studio. Rob was like the Queen and never carried money. That's where the similarities end.

Back in the studio, we recorded some crackers in that session. The one with the All Saint backing vocals was actually the original version of Strong. The day it was written was the day I realised just how talented Robbie was as a writer. I think the general consensus was that Guy wrote everything and Rob threw in a few cheeky rhymes, but as I watched them constructing the track it became clear that the majority of it was already in Rob's head and Guy's genius lay in how he found a way of deconstructing it and putting it into chords and melody. It was like Love is shit all over again. Another great track we recorded in that session was a version of The Pet Shop Boys 'I Wouldn't Normally Do This Kind Of Thing' with legendary producer, CLANG! ... STUART EPPS. He was most famous for producing most of the early Elton John songs, when he was good, and still had some of his own hair (Elton, not Stuart). Lovely man. I learnt a lot from him. Do you remember that episode of Friends? The one with the 'Routine'? Ross and Monica having a dance off. One of my proudest moments is that the music playing when they enter the club is that track. I think that deserves a, CLANG! ... FRIENDS. ALL 6 OF THEM and Oh... My... God... not forgetting Janice.

One afternoon, when I was at home in the Staines massive, I received a call. The man introduced himself as Bob, a reporter for The Sun newspaper. He asked if I would be interested in giving him a couple of Robbie Williams related stories in exchange for fifteen thousand pounds. I said I wasn't interested, and he instantly upped his offer to twenty-five thousand. I again refused. 'Nothing too damning.'

he said, 'Just a couple of off the record quotes. I wont even name you.' I told him there wasn't enough money in Guy Chambers wallet that would get me to spill the beans. 'GOOD ANSWER.' replied Robert Peter Williams, sneakily, from the other end of the phone. The story goes that Rob tried the same gag on everyone in the band and crew, and somebody did spill. Never found out who. You can't get much with twenty-five grand these days anyway can you?

South of the Border had charted, once again, slightly disappointingly, and Life Thru A Lens had come out to mixed reviews, and initial poor sales. It was a worrying time, summed up by Guy Chambers himself, as we sat in the BBC studios the afternoon of our appearance on The National Lottery. He said he was worried that Rob's record deal wouldn't get extended if the album sales didn't pick up. It was at this point that I pointed out something that went a long way to the future success of both Robbie and Guy. One word. Six letters. Beginning with A and ending in NGELS.

We were just starting the promo run for it, as it was coming out as a single just before Christmas. That evening, as we mimed to eight million people on a Wednesday evening, just before the balls dropped, I witnessed the power of the track. It had magical powers, especially when it hit the solo after the second chorus and then smashed into the final 'and through it all, she offers me protection'. I'd played it to my Dad about three months previously, before anyone had heard it, and he had said it was going to be a smash hit, and sure to send Robbie into the showbiz stratosphere. He also asked me to invite him round to his house for a BBQ because he thought they would get on well. Bless him. My Dad's ace. He has seen me play for everyone over the years. No one could have been more supportive than him and my Mum. It's down to them that I do what I do today.

The Angels promo was a real bucket list ticker. Next day, This Morning with, CLANG! ... RICHARD &, CLANG! ... JUDY. They were morning telly royalty back in 1997. Like Phillip Schofield & Holly Willoughby are today. They used to sit in two chairs, with the River Thames flowing behind them, and had an engaging way of interviewing their guests. Before we were due on, we were just milling around, waiting; when it came to commercial break time. R&J got up and went to their respective bathrooms, for a comfort break, during their three minute window of opportunity. Robbie and I decided it would be a brilliant idea to sit in their chairs and do some presenting of our own. Everyone laughed. The cameramen laughed. The producers laughed. On his return Richard laughed. On her return Judy didn't. With a face like thunder like someone who had found out that there was no more chardonnay in the fridge, she bluntly told me to get the f**k out of her chair. Ironic really that five minutes later Rob was miming the words 'I sit and wait'.

The promo bandwagon rolled across Europe once again, taking in TFI Friday, and Top of The Pops (twice). A trip to Paris, where we played in the round like the Beatles, all in white, with flowers on the floor; this was followed by a very scary scenario in Italy. The fans out there are proper bonkers, in a lovely way, and wherever we went they were there in their hundreds. After a TV show, there were so many fans outside that security were really stumped as to how to get Rob out of the building. There were definitely elements of Beatlemania. He just shrugged and said it happened everyday in Take That. It didn't to me. After a series of discussions involving men whose arms were bigger than my thighs, it was agreed that the best way to get him out safely was to put one of us under a blanket and race us through the baying crowd to the awaiting van whilst Rob was escorted out of another door into the back of an old post office van and join us a mile up the road. A superb plan, unless you're the unlucky nominee to be under the blanket. So, thirty seconds later, I was huddled under a blanket surrounded by Sly Stallone and his mates and as they said go, my feet didn't touch the ground until I was hurled into the back of a mini bus and told to keep my head down and under the blanket amid the sound of pubescent Italians screaming. It was pretty scary stuff, but not as scary as the next incident.

We had convened at the bottom of a hill to meet the post office van and collect our singer. All safely tucked into the minibus and, once again, a complete band, we took off toward our hotel. Out of nowhere, suddenly, came scooters from all angles, all with two riders, one steering, and one with a very large camera pointed in our direction. The Italian Paps were after a picture and were determined to get it. Our driver was a very cool looking dude in dark glasses, with that long, lush, thick hair only Italians have. Hair envy at its most prevalent. He pulled on a pair of expensive looking driving gloves, not like Alan Partridge, more like Jackie Stewart. He then popped a cocktail stick into the side of his handsome jaw line and told us to hang on tight. OMG, I have never been so scared in all my life. He must have driven at 100mph, swerving around corners, and flying up side streets. It was like an episode of Starsky & Hutch. Mad Bastard. By the time we flew into our hotel car park he had lost all of the mopeds, and nearly lost

Britain's favourite light entertainer, and Muff Sandwich. Now that would have been a headline for the front pages.

## CHAPTER 15
## ... MYSTIC GAZ

While we were in Europe on the Angels promo run, Rob and I were heavily into our backgammon. We literally played every spare moment we had. One day in a European country which I can't remember the name of, I was on a proper hot streak. I was kicking his pop star arse. He was getting a little flustered at this scenario and the band and crew around us were all aware. We took a break and when we later sat down for another session, we opened the lid and there was a small piece of paper with the words 'Chris Sharrock 01967554672'. The whole room burst out laughing as did I.

Chris Sharrock, as well as being my favourite drummer, was then and still is now, had played the drums on Life Thu a Lens, and was currently on tour with World Party. This may not seem relevant at this point, but in about ten minutes reading you'll see the comic irony. World Party, for the uninitiated, were, and still are, a band fronted by the mighty Karl Wallinger. I love that band. She's the One, a huge hit for Robbie, is a World Party song.

Through a mutual friend I got to meet, CLANG! ... KARL WALLINGER once, at midnight, at his studio in London. He had previously been in another of my favourite bands, The Waterboys, so, under the whole of the moon, I rang the bell to the studio and, after many flights of stairs, was greeted by the man himself. We chatted for hours and it was fascinating to get his take on music, studios, recordings, songs, song writing, production, and, probably, football. A real night to remember. It's still strange to meet your heroes, even if you meet them in the capacity of working with them.

I got to audition for The Waterboys several years later. It was a fantastic experience. CLANG! ... MIKE SCOTT. I walked into the studio and there he was. Just the same as I had seen him, countless times, live and on TV. He was obsessed with Strummer, and kept asking me questions about my time with Joe. We played through some Waterboys songs, with him and the band, and although it never went any further, it was a real musical highlight for me. Auditions can be tough. They are musical job interviews. Nerve wracking, and, also, strangely unnerving, as you are coming face to face with people you have watched, and usually admired, so many times on TV.

I remember auditioning for Squeeze. That started after a Robbie gig somewhere. I was in the dressing room afterwards with David Enthoven and a man with glasses, who turned out to be, CLANG! ... CHRIS DIFFORD. He complimented me on my drumming and after a nice chat he left. I said to David what a nice chap he was, and he just laughed and said, 'You haven't a clue who he is have you?' Anyway, a few moons later, and I was asked to go to, CLANG! ... GLENN TILBROOK's studio to audition for Squeeze. He was an incredible ball of energy, bouncing from wall to wall like a hyperactive teenager. We recorded two songs; one I remember being called 'I Lost The Childen'. No idea why I remember that. Anyway, the next morning I got a phone call. 'Smiley, it's Glenn. Here's the deal. Difford wants you, I want Ash Soan.' (for those of you not in the drumming world you've probably seen Ash on ITV's The Voice. Terribly handsome, with a tidy shuffle. Great drummer and lovely chap. I digress. 'I'm gonna toss a coin', said Tilbrook in his cheeky cockney Squeezy voice. 'By the way, the first gig is in Bermuda. Heads or tails?' I went with my head. Should have gone with my dog instinct.

Another strange audition was for, CLANG! ... MARK OWEN. It consisted of me, Mark, and his MD, Mike Stevens, sitting in a room with them saying, 'We know how you play, can you start Thursday week?' That was that then. I was Mark Owen's drummer. Although, by the time Wednesday week had come, I hadn't heard anything so, actually, I wasn't. Turns out, a shorter, and far more handsome, drummer had walked in directly after me and was now in the drum seat. Damn you tallness! The Lord giveth and the Lord taketh away.

Another time, I received a phone call. Would I be up for a world tour with, CLANG! ... THE EURYTHMICS. Obviously, I excitedly answered with a big fat 'Yes'. Emails were exchanged, tours dates confirmed, passport details sent. I was all ready to tour the world with Annie and Dave. Then one more email. 'They have decided to go with a more urban looking band.' That freed the diary up instantly. About eighteen months of it.

Next one. CLANG! ... BRYAN FERRY. Would I be up for recording drums on his new album. Of course. He was a Roxy Music legend. Dates were booked. Pre-production discussed on the Monday. Email to confirm studio details on the Tuesday. On Wednesday Bryan, apparently, throws his album in the bin, after deciding to record a 1920's musical instead. Either the shittest excuse ever, or a dramatic change in musical direction. I'll let you decide. There were others. Some

I got, some I didn't. As I say, auditions are like job interviews, and buses.

It was Christmas time, and the Muff Sandwich lads were called into a studio in North London to record a Robbie Williams original Christmas song. On the way there I was so excited. I felt like Noddy Holder. Surely from now on Christmas Day around the in-laws would be spent eating turkey, playing games and people saying 'You're on the radio again Smiley'. Lovely. PRS payouts paying for the crackers every year. Sadly, the Christmas classic was not one of Rob's finer hours. The track, 'Walk This Sleigh', was Rob in typical piss taking form. He laughed, we laughed. The record company didn't. That was that. We were lined up to do Top of The Pops, but it was cancelled at the last minute. All I remember about that was that there was a rehearsal for it, and Guy asked me to bring a percussionist. I got my best mate Si to do it. He wasn't really a percussionist, he was a headmaster, but he was a brilliant blagger. I remember it because Rob gave him some shoes. I got a pair too. Rob's Mohair Gucci's. I remember thinking they might be worth something in years to come. Twenty years later when I was clearing out my garage, I found them. Even the biggest Robbie fan would have struggled to put on a smiling face when presented with a pair of mouldy rotting size nine's, previously worn by their hero. They were binned, and soon afterwards, so was I.

In January 1998, I received a lovely letter from Tim and David thanking me for the time I had spent with Rob after shows etc during his post rehab time, and how happy they were with me and Muff Sandwich. What a lovely gesture I thought. In February 1998, the production manager called on a

Monday morning to tell me we would be doing The Brits on Thursday, with Robbie dueting with, CLANG! ... TOM JONES. Now that was one to tell my Mum straight away. That day was filled with an air of excitement and anticipation as I listened to 'It's not unusual', and, 'Land of a 1000 dances', ready for rehearsals on Wednesday. At seven o'clock the phone rang in my lounge and it was Tim Clarke. It's funny what you remember isn't it. I remember his opening line like it was yesterday. 'Smiley it's Tim, I'm afraid I have some rather bad news'. I was then told the news that Guy had decided he wanted Chris Sharrock in the band (told you there was a relevance ten minutes ago). Tim said he and David were extremely sorry about the situation. Even in a heartbreaking moment like that, Tim is still one of the loveliest people I have ever met. We finished our conversation and I put the phone down. Within the next few hours, I had received calls from members of the band, the crew, and the management. Then Guy called. He explained that he needed Chris with him as they were best friends. He thanked me, complimented me on my playing, then jokingly told me that it was costing a small fortune to bring in the new drummer. I didn't laugh. I'd kind of had enough by then. One more call. Shall I just ignore it? I picked up. It was Robbie. He was lovely. What he said will stay between us, but I was touched by his words. The next day I received a call to go to the management to pick up something. Sitting there was a beautifully gift-wrapped package, a Backgammon board from Asprey's, probably worth more than my Fiat Uno, with my name engraved in gold. It was from Rob. Two days later I sat, along with eleven million others, watching Robbie and Tom Jones owning the Brits. It was an emotional night, one I will never forget, because while Rob and Tom were shaking their tail feathers, my mate Fraser was

MOTing my car at the end of the garden, shouting 'brake pads are shot mate.' As I say, it's amazing what you remember.

Over the decades that followed I stayed on great terms with everyone involved with Rob's superstardom. Tim and Dave would throw work my way, and would always make me feel super welcome whenever I went to concerts. I remember going to Wembley Arena for a show. Backstage afterwards, Wob Roberts, the production manager, asked me to follow him to a small room. In it was a beautiful acoustic guitar. He pulled out a black marker pen. 'Rob's gone home and I need this signing' He pointed out that I used to share Rob's signing duties as I knew how to do his autograph. Wrong I know, but hey, sue me. I dutifully signed the guitar. The next day whilst watching MTV, the presenter told the viewers of an exciting competition for all Robbie Williams fans. First prize, a beautiful acoustic guitar, signed by his old drummer.

I kept in touch with Rob, via the management and various get togethers over the years. The last hook up was in 2016, at David Enthoven's funeral. The eulogy, given by Tim, was perfect, summing up a superhuman life lived to the full. He was a wonderful man David, and I miss him terribly. Rob wore a pink suit and sang at the service. I managed to get a few minutes alone with him afterwards, which was lovely. He told me he loved my music. I told him how proud I was of him and that fatherhood had made him 'One of Gods better people'.

## CHAPTER 16
## … SPORT

Never trust a man who doesn't like football. It's weird, and, more than likely, so will he be. Football, and sport in general, are integral to music, to bands and fans alike. There's nothing better than being away from home on tour and being crowded around a laptop with the internet cutting in and out, trying to watch your team being battered in front of your band mates, whose teams are having a brilliant afternoon, and having their loving arms reaching out for you in your hour of need. Football is the logical ice breaker. The opening gambit in any situation. An audition, meeting a celebrity, new work colleagues. You can cut through the ice with a well placed 'Port Vale played well Saturday'. Even if someone isn't a true blue, goner, Geordie, or saint, they will more than likely have at least a tenuous allegiance to a club, even if it's via a distant relative or a close friend. If someone dismisses the subject out of hand with a 'Don't like football', then avoid them at all costs.

My family have been footy mad all our lives. Chelsea runs blue through my Dad's side from generation after generation. I fought it in my early teens, and pretended to be a Man Utd fan, but my Dad wasn't having any of it and continued taking me to Stamford Bridge on regular occasions. Christmas time would often be planned around a trip to the footy with my late Grandfather and assorted Uncles and Cousins. My Dad even used to take me on a rainy Wednesday school night, with Chelsea playing against teams like Wrexham and Nottingham Forest. This was well before the Russian money arrived. My Dad was always brilliant at the footy. He would sing along with all the songs but, being a pastor, always swerve the swear words. His versions of 'What the flipping heck was that' and 'Who's the banker in the black' were legendary. The last time I went with him was 2018. He was in his season ticket seats. After sitting down, four burly blokes behind us lent in and asked if I was the drumming one of his three sons. After the confirmation, they burst into a gutsy and very loud version of The Alarm classic 'Sixty Eight Guns'. I was half flattered and half embarrassed. My Dad joined in. Then I was embarrassed. Football fans, for the most, are a good humoured bunch of piss takers. Take away the small minority of knobhead's, and most stadiums are full of top banterers. I took my mate Dale Davis to Stamford Bridge last year. Dale's a massive Arsenal fan, and also a big piss taker, so I knew he'd fit in. As we took our seats, I introduced him to the Chelsea fans seated around us. This is Dale, he's a Gooner. That was a fun filled ninety minutes.

In my early teens, after I had gone through my stupid Man U period, myself and some of the lads from school would get on the 237 bus from Sunbury Cross to Shepherds Bush, where we would go see QPR. They were shit. They still are. That didn't put us off, and it became quite a fun adventure until we were chased by some scary looking Crystal Palace fans, who seemed quite upset about Vince Hilaire's disallowed volley. I hid under a hedge in someone's garden. For an hour and a half, just to be sure. We then changed our Saturday afternoon team to Brentford. A much nicer club, more enjoyable football. I still have an allegiance to them now courtesy of my dear friend and Hard Fi frontman, CLANG! ... RICHARD ARCHER, as well as the, legendary, Audience co founder and all-round good egg, CLANG! ... BILLY REEVES. He is one of my clever friends. A brilliant mind, he has an exquisite view on politics, as well as being a commentator for Radio London at all the Brentford matches. If you text him song titles during the match, he will drop it into the commentary. Brilliant. 'The Brentford keeper standing tall there, like a Bat Out Of Hell', and 'great work down the right there, the ball in looked like it would Rock The Casbah'. When I had my solo albums out, he would drop the titles in. How he got 'Smileys Friends in Far out places' into Brentford v Notts County I will never know. Football was always the constant in our youth. Me, Dad and my brothers would spend hours every Sunday afternoon over the park firing crosses in for each other to attempt an outrageous bicycle kick. We would only stop when my Mum reminded my Dad that he was preaching at six. Every day after school would be spent in the park with mates playing till the sun went down. Jumpers for goalposts? Isn't it, wasn't it, marvellous.

Playing for your school team was a real badge of honour. I can remember playing number nine for Kenyngton Manor. I can still remember the goals I scored, and the misses I missed. They are just etched into your brain. My Dad came to every match. He even started driving us to matches as he had a big van. When we reached the cup final back in 1979 it ended two all. That meant a penalty shootout. It's a very nervewracking experience when you're eleven. Luckily my Dad was there to help. 'Let my boy go first. He's bound to score'. I missed. We lost. Cheers Dad. In my teen years I played for some legendary clubs. Sunbury Spurs, Haliford Colts. All the greats. I even got transferred to Sunbury Celtic for two Curly Wurlys and a tracksuit top. It was controversial at the time, as it meant Neil Cook went the other way in the deal. Not quite Fernando Torres and Andy Carroll I grant you, but it was big news at Sunbury Manor

Comprehensive. They were great years. I carried on playing till my early thirties, by that point it was five-a-side on a Monday night, until a tricky little winger tackled me from the side and took out my right knee. That was the end of my football career. A sad day for everyone involved in the sport.

Some of the best clangs have come through the football/music connection. You see, all footballers want to be musicians and vice verse. We had some brilliant visitors in dressing rooms over the years. Let me see, CLANG! ... STUART PEARCE. He was a huge Jam fan, and I bent his ear for ages after a show in Nottingham. CLANG! ... CHRIS WADDLE. Again a huge Jam fan, but the difference between him and Psycho was about eight pints. He could hardly stand up, but loved showing us how well he could sing, at the top of his geordie voice. You would have thought 'Diamond Lights', his duet with Glenn Hoddle from back in the day would have given him a nudge in the 'you're a bit shit Chris' direction, but it clearly hadn't. I remember him singing 'Down in the tube station at midnight' with, CLANG! ... BRUCE FOXTON, behind him, mouthing the words 'Get him out of my f*****g dressing room'. Howay the lad.

The biggest and best name drop football/music combo came at a party in London. It was something to do with, CLANG! ... JOE STRUMMER (Joe's name will be mentioned countless times in the upcoming chapters, so I'll leave his clang here.) Anyway, I was talking to, CLANG! ... MANI, from The Stone Roses. He's a massive Man Utd fan, and when I told him, CLANG! ... ERIC CANTONA, was sitting in the corner, he nearly exploded with excitement. We agreed to go and say hello together. Safety in numbers. Eric was surrounded by wide eyed hangers on, and we queued to see him, like the line waiting for Santa's grotto in Debenhams in December. We finally got to the front. I was first. He looked at me. I looked at him. I held out my hand. He shook it. I walked away. Job done. Three hours later, Mani was still in his ear. They are still mates now, apparently. That's the thing about meeting genuine superstars. It's surreal.

I sat on a plane once in 2000, from Japan to New Zealand. No idea why I was in Business class, but I was. An enormous mountain of a man sat next to me. After making sure we weren't sitting on each other's seat belts, we got chatting. I explained that I was on tour with Joe Strummer, and we were flying to New Zealand and Australia for the Big Day Out Festival, along with, CLANG! ... ,THE RED HOT CHILI PEPPERS, FOO FIGHTERS, BLINK 182, and, PRIMAL SCREAM. He was well impressed. After a few of my hilarious Rock & Roll stories, and several bloody mary's I enquired of my new friend's occupation. 'I'm a wrestler' he replied. Well I had never met a real-life wrestler. I remembered my Grandad watching World of Sport every Saturday afternoon. Big Daddy, Giant Haystacks, Mick McManus. Great memories. He definitely wasn't like any of them. 'What's your name' I asked the 6ft 7 Maori handsome giant next to me. CLANG! ... 'THE ROCK', he replied. I wonder what he ended up doing with his life.

Bizarely after saying goodbye to my new pal, CLANG! ... DWAYNE JOHNSON, I boarded another plane a week later, from New Zealand, bound for Australia. I was joined by another sporting hero called Johnston. This time, CLANG! ... CRAIG JOHNSTON. The former Aussie Liverpool striker, who spent the journey telling me about his new vocation, a football boot he was trying to patent with Adidas called 'The

Predator'. He even pulled a prototype out of his bag. It looked like a big black rubber shark fin. Again, I wonder what happened to him, and his funny looking boots.

Now then; Cricket. There's a sport that divides opinion. It's like marmite. No one ever says, 'I quite like it'. You're either in or out. I was lucky to have an Australian best friend. He gave me such an open opinion on the sport back in our living together phase. I remember being in Australia with him, when The Ashes were on. We were playing golf and after our round we went into the bar. England were a tidy 94 for 1. I pumped my sunburnt shoulders out and ordered the beers. Mick said at the top of his voice 'This is Steve, he's a Pom'. Everyone in the bar came over and gave my hand a friendly shake. What a lovely bunch I thought. So gracious. Then they pulled up chairs and gathered round me in front of the TV. What I didn't know was that the cricket was on tape as the barman had recorded it for all the golfers while they were out on the course. Turns out they all knew what was coming in the next hour, as Shane Warne ripped through the English batting line up like a scene from the movie 'Twister'. My new Aussie friends helped me through this tricky time with consolatory beers. They're a caring bunch.

Aussie Mick had an incredibly positive way of looking at cricket, and sport in general. I've come to realise that it's a real Aussie trait. I hope I have adopted that attitude in the way I watch sport. Basically, I learnt to be a good loser. You get that being a Chelsea fan ha ha. Cricket was always huge in our house growing up, and it dictated all of our family holidays in the Channel Islands. While my Sis and my Mum would go off looking for lovely craft shops or collecting shells, Me, Dad and the twins would set up a cricket pitch on the beach, which usually covered about a 150 yard range, and basically bowl, bat and field for hours.

There was a beautiful old church on the picturesque Island of Herm, just off the coast of Guernsey. We used to holiday there and one balmy summer evening, the beaches were clear, apart from four cricketers bombing around shouting 'four' a lot. I was batting, and managed to connect with a ball with perfect symmetry in every way. It sailed over the hill and into the courtyard behind. Off we went, ball searching. After about an hour we were still ball less. Then, as we stood in the twilight, my Dad was looking at the stained glassed window above the church door. It was a stunning piece of art depicting the last supper. There was Jesus and all his disciples, breaking bread and turning the water in wine. What we hadn't spotted in the top left corner was a hole the size of a cricket ball. After finding said cricket ball laying under one of the church pews, a family consultation was called. The fam were split on, keeping schtum, and sneaking off without saying anything, or paying a potential arm and leg for a replacement, once original, and now with added cricket ball hole, stained glass window. The other side of the argument, or as it's better known, my Dad's, was shorter and to the point. 'I'm a pastor'. Honesty prevailed as he went to the keepers of this beautiful building and confessed our guilt. The Lord, and the Herm church association, praised his honesty and in the name of the Lord, let us off. There's a lesson in that story for everyone. It is simply, 'move further down the beach when you're playing cricket'. Amen.

They were some of the best times of my life, on those golden Guernsey beaches. In 2018 I had the pleasure of playing drums on, CLANG! ... MARK BUTCHER's album. He is a former England test batsman, who now commentates for Sky, but is also a brilliant singer songwriter. He's also a top bloke, and I love messaging him during England matches, asking his opinion. He's like a wise old cricketing owl. Always right. Maybe I should start popping a few bets on now I have insider knowledge. It's brilliant knowing sportsmen; it gives you such an incredible insight into their world. I'm good mates with former Wimbledon footballer, CLANG! ... STEWART CASTLEDINE. He was a member of the famous 'Crazy Gang', with Vinnie Jones and Dennis Wise. He tells a brilliant story, and as a bonus is married to 'Homes Under The Hammer' presenter, CLANG! ... LUCY ALEXANDER. What's not to like in that house? His fabulous old stories of Vinnie and Den; and her take on how the downstairs loo should be painted.

Another great sport shared by friends and acquaintances is golf. Yes golf. The tiny little white ball you hit with big sticks toward a tiny hole four hundred yards away and you only get four hits. Stupid annoying game most of the time, exhilarating on that rare occasion you have a good day at the office. One of the most bizarre showbiz stories revolves around golf. A few years ago, I got asked to play in a Pro Celebrity tournament in Surrey. My mate Mickey had put me up for it and when I arrived, I was warmly hugged by the host, CLANG! ... JEREMY KYLE. Now I was touched at Jezza's embrace and, surreally, was present when he received a phone call to say he had landed a morning show on ITV that would make him a household name. After Jez had stopped punching the air and shouting 'Yes!! Get in!!', I asked about the golf day. He explained it was made up of teams of four, and each group had a celebrity in it. How exciting I thought. Who was our celeb? I looked around. I spotted, CLANG! ... PAT SHARP. Then I gave a little, fellow golfer, nod to, CLANG! ... IAN WRIGHT. This was getting better by the minute. I saw Mickey. 'Who's our celeb then Mick?', 'You are' he replied. How disappointing. How disappointing for the other three. They wanted Pat Sharp. They must have been bloody short of celebs if I was one of them. 'Oh well' I thought, what's the worst that can happen. 'Ladies and Gentlemen, welcome to our honourary charity celebrity golf day, and teeing off first, for the blue team, former Robbie Williams drummer, Smiley'. If ever I had wished I'd stuck to lift engineering, it was now as I moved towards the first tee in front of about eighty golfers and handful of, pretty piss poor, celebrities. It's a funny old game this celebrity lark. FORE!

# CHAPTER 17
## ... DOES THAT GET ON THE CV?

1998. A year of what we will call, musical odd's and sod's, but with some whopping Clangs. I got a call to go and play drums on an EP for a band called 'Vega 4'. We met at a studio somewhere I can't remember. What I do remember is the singer. He had a real star quality about him. Piercing eyes, dark lush hair (instant hair envy) and a thick Irish accent. His name was Johnny. His songs were brilliant. His band were ace. They were close to being signed and he clearly had the musical bit between his teeth. The recording went well, and John was keen for me to join permanently. I was happy to, but had other irons in my fire, and the question of commitment was brought up. It's a tricky situation being a 'session' musician. Original bands can be very demanding about loyalty. It's a scenario that has come up all across my career. After some lengthy discussions it was decided 'Vega 4' would appoint a full time, non session drummer, focused purely on them. I had the recording under my belt, and we left on good terms.

Last year I was in a studio in Woking, visiting my friend Richard. He told me there was an old friend of mine who I hadn't seen for many years in the neighbouring studio. The old friend turned out to be the drummer who replaced me in 'Vega 4'. His name escapes me. Nice chap. I knew the history of the band, the typical, 'close but no cigar', story. As I remember, they were together for about five years and then it was all over. 'Whatever happened to Johnny? Did he ever do anything exciting?' He looked at Richard, and they both smiled. Then it dawned on them I was asking a serious question. 'Did he ever do anything exciting?, apart from forming, CLANG! ...

SNOW PATROL, and marrying, CLANG! ... COURTNEY COX.'

Yes folks, my old mate, CLANG! ... JOHNNY McDAID, had married Monica from Friends, and formed one of the biggest bands on the planet, as well as writing for everyone from Ed Sheeran to Robbie. My mate Dave White works for Sheeran and I asked him. 'Oh, John's a good mate of mine, I'll ask him if he remembers you, next time I see him. Turns out he does, but never really forgave me for my session like betrayal of his band. Shame, I would have happily double dated with Rachel.

My mate Jeff Ward, who I mentioned earlier in the book, the one who had the studio in Staines etc. Anyway, he had moved to a little place in Ireland called Clonakilty. He had set up a studio in his house on the top of a hill. The nearest neighbour was over two miles away. It was stunning. The view stretched for miles, as did the silence. It was after recording all day there, that I realised my hearing was starting to get worse. Anyone who knows me will tell you I'm a little bit deaf, and if it's my wife or kid's sharing this little snippet, they'll probably laugh while telling you. The silence, as they say, was deafening. So was the tinnitus. I remember, CLANG! ... ZAK STARKEY, asking me at, CLANG! ... CHESNEY HAWKES' wedding about it, as he was suffering with the same problem. I've since found that tinnitus is controllable and that's why, ever since that showbiz wedding, Zak, myself, and any other sensible drummer, will always wear, either, in ear monitors, or ear plugs.

Anyway, back to Ireland, and Jeff was producing a bit of a living legend. CLANG! ... ROY HARPER. He was a very famous folk singer, back in the day, and a big mate of Led Zeppelin, so much so that the band have a song called 'Hats Off To Roy Harper', on the album Led Zeppelin 3. Roy was an incredible man. He was also mad as a box of frogs. We used to record and then sit and watch the cricket together. He also lived on a hill in the middle of nowhere. One night after a long day of recording, cricket and tinnitus, he asked me if I had ever seen a UFO. My answer was no. Now, Clonakilty is near Cork, which apparently is the UFO capital of the world. Roy smiled and said I would 'believe' at midnight. At eleven-fifty-eight he took me out to his back garden, and, in the deathly silence, pointed out a bright star-like light in the middle of the sky. He then pointed to two more, one on the far left, the other on the far right. 'Watch the two wide lights' he instructed. They both slowly started moving toward the middle light. After about two minutes, left light and right light disappeared into middle light, then, WHOOSH, middle light shot up at warp speed and, bang, was gone. 'That happens every night at midnight' Roy said 'They are watching us. I've even seen a spaceship come out of the lake'. If I hadn't seen it for myself, and heard the story from an eccentric old folk singer in a bar, I wouldn't have given it a second thought, but I did see it. Twice, with an eccentric folk singer, in his garden.

Jeff was also working with, CLANG! ... NOEL REDDING. Noel was the bass player in the Jimi Hendrix experience. He had semi-retired to the Irish countryside, but was recording an album, with Jeff producing. I was asked to play drums on one track, an old track that he wanted to resurrect. I dutifully turned up at the studio the next day, recorded the track, and then played live that night with Noel, Jeff, and a handful of fabulous old, slightly pissed, local Irish musicians. As I flew home the following day, I knew this wonderful place would always be special to me, and I've been out several times since, recording, and playing shows.

Years later, I saw Jeff in a pub in Staines, where he was visiting his Dad. He said he had an exciting thing to tell me. I ordered us a couple of beers and sat down. 'You remember that track you drummed on for Noel Redding?' he said. 'You remember it was an old track he had redone?' 'Yes Jeff, and your point?'. 'Well, Noel found the original guitar track and used it on the new recording. You're on a track with, CLANG! ... JIMI HENDRIX'. Now, I know musicians who would have used that on their CV without blinking, but I thought having Hendrix wedged in between Chesney Hawkes and Matt Goss on mine might be pushing it a bit; but, technically, I was in the Jimi Hendrix experience, 'ish. That's good enough for me.

As I've mentioned already, musical CV's are a proper grey area. I was in a studio in London recording for a band not particularly worthy of a clang, and in the studio next door was a producer I knew. At lunchtime he told me he was doing a remix for, CLANG! ... THE CHARLATANS. He asked me to put some drums on the track, and so, when the unclangable's had popped out for lunch, I nipped next door and laid down the drums. Now, as far as I know, the remix never came out. So, here's the question. Do The Charlatans make my CV?

CLANG! ... LILY ALLEN. When Lily was about 15, she hung around Strummer world, with her crazy dad Keith. She even got on stage with us at Wembley Arena when we were supporting, CLANG! ... THE WHO. A few years later, Pablo was producing one of her tracks 'Gay Icon'. He asked me to play drums on it, and as a friend, and as her Dad was paying, the drums were done. Now, I’ve never seen that track on any of Lily's albums since she made it big, but does she still slip onto the CV?

Another similar scenario was putting drums on a, CLANG! ... ALEXANDRA BURKE, track; a version of Live And Let Die, for my producer friend, Ash Howes. It was a brilliant version, but I've never heard it since. Ash also got me on a track by, CLANG! ... NEWTON FAULKNER. A brilliant song, called 'Passing Planes'. I've since heard it, and it’s a dance mix. So, is Newton still on the CV? Great game this isn't it. Similar scenerio for live appearances. I've done shows where a 'Special Guest' will get up and sing one song. I've had that with, CLANG! ... SIA, CLANG! ... MATT GOSS, CLANG! ... PHIL DANIELS, CLANG! ... SIMON FOWLER (OCEAN COLOUR SCENE), CLANG! ... GLENN MATLOCK (SEX PISTOLS), CLANG! ... STEVE NORMAN (SPANDAU BALLET), CLANG! ... BILLY DUFFY (THE CULT), CLANG! ... DENNY LAINE (WINGS), CLANG! ... TERRY HALL (THE SPECIALS), CLANG! ... CAPTAIN SENSIBLE, and, CLANG! ... BILLY CORGAN (SMASHING PUMPKINS).

If you add all those, and they are all a hundred per cent true, the old CV isn't looking too shabby.

OK! Magazine 1997 ... one for my Mum.

Robbie United v The Supernaturals. Germany 1997.

With the Backgammon king!

Olympia Theatre, Dublin 1997. One of my favourite venues.

Elysée Montmartre, Paris 1997. Another favourite venue.

Joe Strummer and the Mescaleros
1999. Studious legend.

New York 1999. Photograph by
the legendary Bob Gruen.

Joe Strummer and the Mescaleros
2000. Smiling Legend.

Pre Strummer watch

T in the Park, Scotland 1999.
The longest weekend ever!

Joe Strummer and the Mescaleros 2000.

Flea. Australia 2000.

Dave Grohl. Australia 2000. Just before he sacked his wardrobe lady for shrinking his clothes!

Joe Strummer and Paul Weller V2000.

Best photo I ever took!

Topper Headon, Mick Jones, and Billy Bragg. Sunshine Corner Studios 2009.

Glen Matlock and Mike Peters. Wales 2011.

Smiley's Friends with Richard Archer. Always surround yourself with greatness.

Sting. France 2017.

Mark Butcher and Andy Lewis. Two of my faves!

Bicep competition! Bournemouth Fire Station 2014.

Photograph courtesy of © Derek D'Souza.

Chad Smith. Los Angeles 2019

TV's Gareth 'Gaz Top' Jones, Steve Norman of Spandau Ballet, and Q The Music's Kerry Barnard Schultz, at the Houses of Parliament on the occasion of Mike Peters receiving his MBE.

Ice Ice Baby! Vanilla Ice. Los Angeles 2019.

## CHAPTER 18
## ... MEETING JOE STRUMMER

In the early Robbie days, when we were doing promo in Europe, we had two brilliant musicians with us. Martin Slattery and Scott Shields. They went off to America straight after those dates to do an original project. On a quiet Staines morning in early 1999, I got a call from a chap called Anthony Genn. He explained that he was in the studio with, CLANG! ... JOE STRUMMER, (last one I promise) and that the drummer, Ged Lynch, who I had met before, and who is a wonderful drummer and even more wonderful man, had decided to go off to play with, CLANG! ... MARIANNE FAITHFUL. He explained that Martin and Scott were in the equation, and that they had put my name forward. It was arranged for the next day at a studio in Willesden, London.

Now there is a misconception amongst music fans that if you are playing with an artist, you automatically know all their songs, their albums, their history etc. I've explained many a time to an ardent Clash fan that, if you were my age, you missed the punk explosion by about two or three years. I remember the famous Bill Grundy/Sex Pistols TV clip clearly, but I was just a little boy, waiting for Starsky and Hutch to start. I remember being shocked by the swearing and spiky hair. So, my knowledge of all things Clash, and Strummer, were average but not encyclopaedic, like so many others, who I have since met, over the years. In fact, my initial recollection of Joe was that my mate Phil had showed me the cover of his last solo album, 'Earthquake Weather', and that he was standing on a diving board, smoking a cigarette holding his guitar. I obviously knew the big Clash hits; Rock The Casbah, London Calling, Should I

Stay Or Should I Go' etc, but I wasn't what you would call a 'Fan'. So, I phoned Phil and told him. He was seriously impressed. It took a lot to impress Phil, and indeed his brother Steve. You remember them from the earlier chapters when we smashed the light during England v Germany in the 1990 World Cup Semi Final. I was obviously onto something cool.

The next day I drove to the studio, a bit unsure of what I was going to encounter. I pulled up outside the gates and told the intercom I was there to meet Joe Strummer. As the gates slowly opened, a man with a quiff like haircut and cool black leather biker jacket walked towards the car. I recognised him immediately, even without the diving board. 'Hello Joe, I'm Smiley' I said, to the coolest man I had ever met. 'Sure thing,' he said, 'I'm off to get a paper.' A moment of lasting recognition in my little 'famous moments' brain. I parked and went up toward Studio One to be greeted by a lovely Scott and Martin combo of smiles and hugs. Then a heavily tattooed wiry character. 'Pablo Cook, Mr Smiles' he chirped. I liked him immediately. Then a very handsome, dark haired character walked toward me. 'Hi Smiley. I'm Anthony. Come on in.' We had a coffee and chit chatted before Joe walked back in. 'Have you checked the kid out yet' he bellowed. The kid was me, and five minutes later I was sitting behind a kit in the live room about to play along with a track called 'Techno D Day'. It was a belter, and the drums Ged had recorded were superb. It was the trickiest song on the album they were working on, and they threw me in the deep end to see if I could emulate the great drumming.

Ged had been in Black Grape with Martin. I think our paths had crossed during my Robbie days, but I can't remember when or where, but I can remember what a beautiful soul Ged was, and that we had exchanged numbers. I laid the drums down pretty much in the same style he had and went back into the control room. There were nods of congratulations from everyone in the room, apart from Ant, who was on the phone. They played the track back with my drums instead of Ged's and it all sounded pretty damn good. Lot's of nodding heads and winks. Always a good sign. Then Ant leaned back over the mixing desk. 'Ok guys, here's the situation. Ged's tour with Marianne Faithful has fallen through. As the MD, I need to decide whether to keep him on board or bring Smiley in. I'm going over the road to think about it. Smiley, you're done. I'll call you tomorrow', and, with that, he turned and walked out. I picked up my sticks and bag and said my goodbyes. As I turned towards the door Joe walked toward me. He gave me a hug and whispered, 'whatever will be will be'. Normal words from a normal man. Pretty weighty from a legend.

I drove home and did what any decent honest musician should do in that situation. I phoned Ged. We had a great chat and agreed that, whatever the decision, we would remain friends. Watch and learn drummers, and other musicians. That's how you deal with situations like that. I've heard so many stories of people stealing gigs from other musicians, undercutting them, depping for them, and then worming their way in on the back of the generous gesture of putting them forward in the first place. I've known really close friends fall out forever when a dep has been asked to stay in the job. It's happened to me. Any intelligent muso will tell you, if you put someone else into your gig, for whatever reason, and they get asked to stay there, one phonecall explaining the situation will suffice. Sneaking around behind peoples backs and acting innocent when guilty of backstabbing doesn't wash with me and, especially, the Zildjian drinking club. You know who you are, and so do we. Rant Over.

The following morning the phone rang; it was Ant. He told me as he left the studio to get to the house he was staying in, directly over the road, he had decided to stick with Ged. By the time he had crossed the road, he had changed his mind. No idea why, but who was I to argue. I was now a member of, CLANG! ... JOE STRUMMER AND THE MESCALROS.

Another huge SLIDING DOOR moment. Ged went on to play with, CLANG! ... PETER GABRIEL, so honesty clearly prevailed. I was asked to come back to the studio the following day for rehearsals for the upcoming UK tour. I phoned Phil and Steve. The rehearsal songs were put on hold when I arrived, as Joe informed me that there was one more song to be recorded for the new album, and he wanted me to drum on it. The track was called 'Forbidden City; very political, about Tiananmen Square. Fifteen minutes later I was on Joe Strummers new album, 'Rock Art And The X-Ray Style'. The cover to the album was a painting by Joe's avant garde artist pal, CLANG! ... DAMIEN HIRST. He was always hanging around and would often pop up at future shows all over the world.

One time when we were in Austraila, Damien, Joe, and the band were in a bar, when he started doing little drawings on napkins, signing and dating them, and giving them to each of us. Now at that time, probably around 1999, I wasn't completely up to speed with all things Damien Hirst. I knew he was an artist, very cool in art circles, and that he had sawed a big fish in half and put it in a tank of formaldehyde. So, after a few beers, some pissed bloke giving me a napkin with a load of circles on it didn't really register on the, 'Oh Wow' scale, and I threw it in the bin. A few years ago, someone told me that Anthony Genn had had his framed and recently valued at £150,000. I'll just leave that one with you. You can't get much with £150,000 these days can you? Gulp.

We began rehearsing songs from the new album. The connection between the band was instant and it clicked straight away. Joe's new manager came down to peruse his latest client and his band, and after sitting through five or six as yet unheard tunes, he asked if he could hear London Calling. Joe didn't look happy; it was like his current state of mind had been penetrated by his past. He grumbled for a bit, there was tension in the air, and then out of nowhere he started playing the killer opening riff of The Clash classic. Five seconds later, we all crashed in behind him and the roof was literally blown off. Now that is a moment I will never forget. Simon Moran, the new manager, had, four minutes later, a very big smile on his face. We took a break, to watch the famous European Cup final where Man United beat Bayern Munich in injury time. None of us were United fans, but we had all dutifully adopted our English pride against the old enemy and, as Ole Gunnar Solskjaer scrambled Teddy Sheringham's deflection into the back of the net, the room went crazy and I had a Punk legends arms wrapped around my neck as we bounced around the room. Nothing bonds people better than football, especially beating Germany at football. I was now a Mescalero. It was time to go out on tour. First stop ... UK.

## CHAPTER 19
## ... WELCOME TO CHAOS

So, after a few weeks of rehearsals, it was time to go on a UK tour. The set was two thirds new material, with a third of classic Clash songs, making up the hour and twenty minute set. My pedigree in the Phil and Steve camp was at a high, as I'd managed to blag them into rehearsals, and Steve became Joe's personal cigarette roller. The new songs were good, but the Clash songs were epic. Our first show was at The Leadmill in Sheffiield, the same show as my Mock Turtles/Jennifers/Supergrass memory, six years earlier. A good omen.

Now as I've said before, my memory is pretty shocking in many respects, but I am lucky to have people who live for that kind of shit. Anthony Davie being one of them. We met in Japan. He travelled all the way to see us, and was just kind of hanging around during the soundcheck. I said hello and, when I found out why he was there, invited him into the dressing room. He was like a little kid meeting Little Mix for the first time, bless him. Bizarrely, within a couple of months of the meeting, he was known as 'Internet Anthony' and was running the Mescaleroes website.

Anyway, Ant is a walking encyclopaedia of all things Strummer, so I've tapped him up on a few details so no one can query them. I noticed very early on that there was a pretty hardcore following at the shows, as well as in the dressing room. There were quite a few tasty geezers from Manchester who I later found out were, shall we say, quite connected. I remember being in Australia and two of them turning up just to hang out. One of them smiled at me and said to have a peek in his bag. There was a hundred grand in cash sitting there. I've no idea why, I never asked, but I remember him telling me that if I was ever in any trouble to call him and he could 'sort it'. This was long before Peaky Blinders. I haven't had to call in that favour yet but, hey, you never know.

The shows were going really well. The band was on top form, but I soon got my first glimpse of the 'chaos'. You see Joe loved a bit of chaos. He loved to mix things up to create a reaction. A good example was at our first London show. It was going really well, everyone was playing out of their skins and the crowd was loving it. Suddenly, between songs, Joe started shouting at two guys in the fourth row. He then put his guitar down and waded in. The crowd held its breath as he grabbed the two guys by the lapels and yelled at them. The crowd started cheering, like it was in the playground when there used to be a fight. He let go, snarling as he made his way, via two security guards, back up onto the stage. The crowd was going mental, there was a real edge in the air. He grabbed the mike and shouted something about people taking liberties, or along those lines. The mood changed and there was a real sinister feel as the crowd were shouting at the top of their voices. I didn't know what was going on, only that 'Rock the Casbah' was next on my setlist and I had to count it in. He turned around and looked at me. I froze. What was I to do now? He looked me straight in the eye, and winked, with a little smile. Then he turned back to the crowd and shouted, 'Lets rock this joint'; and, one two three four, boom, we blew the roof off. It was then I realised that this Punk Hero was recreating tension and edginess to the proceedings, that took the evening to a different level. It was intimidating, preconceived, and very clever. That was Joe Strummer.

He used to love people. He would interview anyone and everyone. If you know a Clash fan, they will probably have met Joe, and will all say the same thing. He was more interested in you than you were in him. That's when I discovered 'Strummer watch'. After a show, we were back on the bus, ready to depart for the next venue. The tour manager shouted, 'who's on Strummer watch tonight?' 'Smiley!' was the reply. I then found out that the next three hours were spent being interviewed by my new boss on everything from my childhood, religion, politics and football. This also included a bottle of brandy. Over the next few years, I spent many a night travelling across America, deep in conversation with this brilliantly intelligent man, who inspired so many. He also had a real funny side to him. When we played in Belfast one night, a journalist was hanging around desperate to interview him. 'How long do you reckon I can keep him on the bus?' Joe asked the band. 'Place your bets'. When we arrived back in England the next morning, the journalist was still on the bus, drunk as a skunk, and when he finally said he had to be leaving, was let off, unknowingly, a sea crossing away from the Emerald Isle. 'Who had five hours?'

A side of Joe that few saw, was the gentle, emotional, one, that was a million miles away from the snarling Punk Icon. When we played in Germany, we had a night off and, courtesy of the local promotor, went to see The Beach Boys play an outdoor concert. It was lovely to all go as a band and towards the end of the show they played one of my all time favourite songs, 'God Only Knows'. I was sitting in front of the others and halfway through the song turned around to share the moment. I couldn't quite believe my eyes, as Joe and the entire band were sat in tears. You see old Strummer was a bit of a softie on the quiet. I remember having a night off in the South of France once and venturing into town on my own to meet my mate Johnny, who was there on business. I was early, so decided to go for a beer. I walked into a quiet little bar and after getting my pint turned around to find somewhere to sit. There weren't many in the bar, but I did spot Joe, on his own, in the corner. I sat down with him and he immediately put his head on my shoulder and began to cry. It was a lovely shared moment, and after a minute he sat up, rubbed his eyes and apologised. There's never any sorry's involved in a good old cry, even if you are punk legend, and a bit of an old softie. Bless him.

The UK tour was a great success. I was getting to know the band and crew, or so I thought. Now I was aware that there was quite a big drug culture within the touring party. Not Joe so much, but band and crew had their own agendas. It was in Paris that I discovered the extent of them. We were playing the fabulous Elysee Montmartre, a venue I had played with Robbie, and would play many times again, with Archive. I remember being in the dressing room in the afternoon and the tour manager asking the agent if he could get some cocaine. Nothing new there. Not my thing but each to their own. I had decided years before that I wasn't going to try cocaine, for one because I knew I would probably like it, and then goodness knows what would have happened. The other reason was that I had seen too many friends become way too dependent on it, friends who you wouldn't think it would appeal to, whose lives have been seriously affected by that naughty little white powder. So, in the dressing room, the request for a few grams of charlie wasn't that startling. The request for heroin was. I thought he was joking, and sat having a little chuckle. Ten minutes later, as a few of us were having a stroll towards the Eiffel Tower, one of the band stopped me. 'You do know he wasn't joking don't you?' He told me a member of the band was a functioning heroin addict, and had been for years. I was stunned. I was thirty years old and the only knowledge of smack I had was from films, or news articles, or Keith Richards documentaries.

The following day was a day off. We were staying in a rather plush hotel, if I remember rightly. I got a call that the boys were all hanging out in one of the rooms before heading out for food. I got my bits together and went to meet up. As I entered everyone was scattered. I went into the far room and sat at the big dining table. I started chatting with Ant and, after chewing the fat about this and that, he pulled out some tin foil. He tore a sheet off and then took out a small wrap. He opened it and tipped the brown powder onto the foil. You've all seen pictures of someone chasing the dragon, but when someone does it right next to you, while keeping a conversation going, it’s slightly unnerving, especially when he keeps eye contact. If you want to read the full story of his drug addiction, he brilliantly explains it in Anthony Davies' book 'Visions Of A Homeland'. It’s an interesting book, and well worth a read. I saw Ant at David Enthoven's funeral, and he is now clean as a whistle, and writing the music for Peaky Blinders with fellow Mescalero Martin Slattery.

It was good to see him looking so healthy, as we had a chequered relationship during our time on the road together. As much as he was a functioning addict, it did alter his mood, and he would frequently have a little dig at me about certain aspects of my drumming. He was using his title as Musical Director to the full and, one day in Switzerland, he pushed me too far. We came off stage after a storming show, ready to go back on for an encore. Joe sloped off to the toilet and Ant decided to announce, in front of everyone, that he felt my playing had dragged in places. Now I am not arrogant or overconfident as to not be able to take criticism, but, when it's from someone who's been smacked off his tits for half of that week, it's a little too much to take. So I stood up and said he was talking shit. I asked if anyone else agreed and they all put their heads down. I couldn't believe no one stood my ground, and I stormed out of the door and straight back onto the stage, past a slightly startled looking Joe. I was absolutely seething and when we finished the show I walked straight off the stage and was grabbed around the neck by the tour manager. He walked me straight out of the back door and into a bar directly over the road. 'Sit down and calm down' he said, as he went to the bar. He returned with two large brandies and explained how he had heard every word and was taking me out of the situation to save me from saying something I would probably regret in the long term. We stayed for a few hours and put the world to rights until I had calmed down. Now that's great tour management. I'll never forget that Mr Gary Robinson. The next day everybody was over nice and everything calmed down. It never happened again because I think Ant realised he had overstepped the mark. Years later, after coming out of rehab, he wrote me a lovely letter apologising for being out of order to me. I had already forgiven him so that was quite a sweet gesture. It's not easy being in a band, especially when drugs are involved. The craziness had only just begun.

# CHAPTER 20
## ... EVERYBODY WANTS A BIT OF JOE

It was time to hit the festivals. This was a whole new world for me. So, in my new-found, crazy life, within the Strummer bubble, what better place to start than Glastonbury, mainstage. We arrived on the tour bus, and I remember seeing Glasto for the first time. It was like a small village. We were driven through to the backstage area and informed we were on stage at 4pm. I remember our dressing rooms were next to, CLANG! ... THE MANIC STREET PREACHERS, who caused a right old ruckus by having their own designated toilets. It didn't bother me, but some took real offence. I'll let you work out how they showed their disdain.

Also, there was, CLANG! ... FATBOY SLIM. We happily shared the same lavatory facilities, and I remember telling him what a huge fan I'd been of The Housemartins (He was their bass player as Norman Cook before becoming the superstar DJ). Top bloke old Norman. I went for a walk out into the fields, and couldn't believe the sheer size of it, and how many different aspects of entertainment there was. If someone wanted to see a one-legged dwarf balancing a golden retriever on his head while eating a pot noodle, you were in the right place. I walked into the crowd to look at The Pyramid stage where we would be playing later that afternoon. CLANG! ... BILLY BRAGG, was onstage, and announced to the forty thousand people how excited he was that Joe Strummer was playing at four. The crowd cheered and so did I.

Now, I had done something radical that week. I'd got a tattoo on my upper left arm, my new daughter Georgia's name, in Japanese, in a circle. Having read the early chapters of the book, you know why I say the word radical. The last people I would ever tell would be my Mum and Dad. They didn't need to know. So, at five minutes to four it was absolutely roasting. I couldn't make up my mind what to wear and went for a sleeveless white t-shirt and shorts. I thought nothing of it till I sat down behind my kit and looked to my left to see a BBC cameraman pointing his camera straight at my upper left arm. I recall the conversation I had the following afternoon with my lovely Mum. It went something like this. 'Your Uncle Bill rang yesterday to say you were on the telly. We watched you. We were so proud. What's that on your arm'. If I remember rightly, after I had admitted it was a tattoo her response was 'How long will it be there'. Bless her. She never mentioned it again. If she did ask how many tattoos I had now, I would answer in the style of Hugh Grant. 'Less than David Beckham, more than Kate Middleton'.

Anyway, back to the stage, where we were belting through the songs, forty thousand people singing along to the Clash classics, and everything going swimmingly. Of course, this could only mean one thing. The chaos was approaching. We started playing the Clash song 'Straight to hell'. As Joe prowled around the stage, with the mic stand balanced over his right shoulder, a brave BBC cameraman stood in front of him with the camera close up to his face. Now you don't have to be a rocket scientist to work out what happened next, but to quote Jamie Theakston on BBC2 later that evening 'I don't really think it was appropriate for Joe Strummer to hit that cameraman in the face with his microphone stand. Now, let's take a look at The Lighthouse Family from the dance tent last night'. I never found out what was bugging Joe that day. He certainly wasn't happy, but if you watch the footage back on Youtube, it's still pretty impressive. The backstage area afterwards was chaos. We had, CLANG! ... JARVIS COCKER, and, CLANG! ... KEITH ALLEN, in our dressing room and, twelve hours later they were still there, in body only, as they were, by then, on a different planet. Joe used to love sitting around a campfire at festivals, and he had a huge gathering of stoned worshippers with him. I heard he stayed there for a week. Maybe he was a secret boy scout.

Festivals were always interesting as everyone wanted a piece of Strummer. I remember being backstage at V2000 and, CLANG! ... PAUL WELLER, was sitting outside his dressing room strumming his acoustic guitar. I had to say something. It was the modfather, and he was literally twenty yards away. I approached, like a panther about to attack a crocodile. I got right up to him and he looked up and paused his strumming. What do you say to the man you've idolised since school, the coolest dude on the planet. He looked at me. I looked at him. Then my brain decided it would be a good idea to say 'I live near you'. Yep, that was opening gambit to the legendary Jam frontman. Luckily for me, my brain then decided not to say, 'A town called Staines'. Phew. He asked me who I was with, probably with one eye on security to throw me out. When I said Strummer, his eyes went wide, and he asked if he could meet him. 'Leave it with me Paul, I'll have a word'. Luckily I saw Joe walking towards me, and so I introduced the most famous punk to the most famous mod. My work here was done. There's a famous photo of that moment which I swear I took.

Later, when we were standing side of stage ready to go on, Weller was there with, CLANG! ... NOEL GALLAGHER. Noel clearly had no recollection of our little altercation at The Who show a year earlier, well, why would he? He introduced himself and then as we chatted, he thought he had created the world's funniest joke, which, of course, he'd used on me once before. I was Joe's Drummer. He howled with laughter (again). I pretended to. We were friends again, ha ha. So, no pressure as we walked on in front of twenty thousand people and kicked in with London Calling, with old Paul and Noel watching Joe Strummer & Joe's Drummer. It's funnier if you say it fast.

Another amazing festival we did was the Fuji Rock Festival in Japan. You could actually see Mount Fuji from the stage. It was stunning. It was the night before the show that I had my most Rock & Roll moment as a grown up. All the bands appearing at the festival were staying in the same hotel. There were members of bands all over the place. Ready for a mammoth, CLANG! ... HAPPY MONDAYS, PRIMAL SCREAM, OCEAN COLOUR SCENE, FUN LOVING CRIMINALS, CATATONIA, ZZ TOP, and more. It was a stalkers dream.

Everyone was mingling and it was like a musician's wedding. As people started to file off to bed, I was still pretty much wide awake. I got chatting with, CLANG! ... HUEY MORGAN. Fun loving criminal Huey was a proper laugh. One of the coolest men I had ever met. We hit it off straight away and he introduced me to Sake (for those of you unfamiliar with Sake, it's a Japanese drink. Very alcoholic and will trip you up an hour later if you have too many). Here I was, drinking with Fun loving Huey, when Joe joined us. Huey was proper starry eyed. Wow I thought, these are two proper heavyweights to be sitting drinking with. Then we were joined by, CLANG! ... SHAUN RYDER. Oh yes, Happy Monday Shaun, the biggest caner of them all. So, there I was, drinking Sake with Joe, Shaun, and Huey. I was so out of my depth, but I remember asking someone to take a picture. Sadly, I can't find it, but I swear the moment was true. I remember staggering back to my room and waking up in the middle of the night desperate for some water. I reached across and grabbed the glass next to my bed and took a huge gulp... of sake. That was the last time I ever drank it.

The other recollection of Fuji was that we were due on before ZZ Top, and that they tried to swap slots and Strummer said no. There was a right old rumpus, but he stood his ground, and we went on before the beards. I can also remember CLANG! ... BERNARD BUTLER, having an argument with, CLANG! ... ALAN McGEE, backstage. Bernard was the former guitarist with Suede, but was now solo, and Alan McGee was his record label boss, famous for being the brains behind Oasis. As Bernie and Al exchanged words, I was passing and said to Bern 'You were ace today'. 'See, at least someone liked it,' he screamed at McGee. Happy to help. I told Alan Mcgee that story backstage at a festival in Newcastle in 2019. He shrugged his shoulders and walked off. I'm not buying his book now.

The best festival we ever did was T in the Park in Scotland. Not only was it jam packed with crazy Scots who, lets face it, are always up for a good time, it was also an amazing bill as well. CLANG! ... BLUR, were the headliners. We had met them a few months before, in Amsterdam. They had flown themselves to the festival, and were arguing between them about whose turn it was to fly the plane back. I don't know any other bands who have that argument.

Talking of that Amsterdam show, I was sitting side of stage watching, CLANG! ... THOM YORKE, & CLANG! ... JOHNNY GREENWOOD, from, CLANG! ... RADIOHEAD. What a moment. They started playing Karma Police. I was sitting on a flight case and, as I was about to sing along with the first chorus, an American voice whispered in my ear 'Do you mind if I sit here with you?' I looked up and, as a gentleman, naturally, shifted up to share my flight case with, CLANG! ... ALANIS MORRISETTE. Wasn't that ironic?

Anyway, back to Scotland, and again there were some great bands on that bill. We were on after, CLANG! ... THE STEREOPHONICS. I remember meeting their drummer, CLANG! ... STUART CABLE, in the toilet. He was a lovely man, and our paths would cross in years to come, when he was drumming in the support band on an Alarm tour. He had left the Phonics by then and was such an upbeat chap. Loved his drumming. It was a real shock when he died soon after that tour.

I carried on my Housemartin's loving, when I got to meet, CLANG! ... PAUL HEATON, who was there with, CLANG! ... THE BEAUTIFUL SOUTH. Also there, were our new friends, The Fun Loving Criminals. I've since learnt that if you are on a 'festival run', i.e. you're playing all of the European festivals in a year, you generally see the same bands, as they are probably promoting a new album, so the Crims were with us all the time. Huey was really funny, and charismatic, as well as being a bit dangerous. I was in awe. We hung out and went to see bands together. It was when I told him at the end of the night that I had a headache he said he could sort it. He gave me a little blue pill and told me it would sort me out. It did... for two days. Everyone thought it was hilarious. I walked around like Bez without the maracas. After two days of no sleep I finally dropped. Let that be a warning to you kids. Richard Ashcroft was wrong. Zammo was right.

## CHAPTER 21
## ... AIR MILES

1999. La la la la la la merica. I'd never been. Now I was going to play with a living legend. They loved Joe Strummer in the States. The Clash were massive. It was after the first couple of shows that I really started to realise how iconic Joe was in the eyes of, predominantly middle-aged, slightly overweight, bald, American men. The very moment was when a gentleman identified me as Joe's Drummer (stop laughing Noel) after a show and bowed. Yes bowed. I was astonished and thought he was joking. He wasn't. It was slightly embarrassing. Luckily by my side was the legendary One-legged Tim. Now Tim was a fan who had become mates with Joe. He was, just as it said on the tin. He had lost one leg from the knee down in a motorbike accident. He was very handsome, huge, covered in tattoos and incredibly funny. Apart from that, there was nothing memorable about him.

Anyway, he was on the bus with us, so he kind of became my touring buddy. We went everywhere together, especially, according to him, Baby Gap. (Georgia, my eldest daughter was just a baby at the time). It was like having a minder, with one leg. Having said that, he did use that false leg. He loved to hand it to me when we were on a plane together, much to his amusement. He got me with that gag several times. So, me, my new one-legged bezzie, and the Mescaleros, band and crew, went off in a big tour bus across America.

I remember when we first got to New York. It was mind-blowing, and me and hop-along decided, as we had a day off, that we would set out and walk from one side to the other. Strange decision you might think for a couple with the combined number of legs of three, but he was very nimble, and often beat me running across the street. We decided to go on a boat ride to the Statue of Liberty. We found one but it had just pulled away. Then we heard a big noise, and a whoosh of air blew at us from our right. It was a helicopter. A big sign said, 'Fifty bucks'. Sometimes you just have to go with the moment and, ten minutes later, Tim and I were hovering over the Hudson with the twin towers on our left. An amazing experience. I remember also popping into Kiel's, the famous cosmetics store. I think Tim wanted some cream for his overworked stump. We got chatting to a nice lady who was a big Clash fan. After sorting her some tickets for some free limb cream, I noticed a wall full of baby pictures. She explained that it was a homage to young children whose parents had visited the store. I was in New York earlier this year and my, now twenty-year-old, daughter's picture is still on the wall.

That night we played an amazing show, and it was then I noticed some pretty heavyweight celebrities were starting to come to say hello in our dressing rooms. That night, I got introduced to, CLANG! ... MATT DILLON. He was dating Cameron Diaz at the time but, sadly, didn't bring her. Another time in New York, there was a knock at the dressing room door. Some of the band were otherwise engaged in a particularly tricky activity and asked me to check who it was. I opened the door and standing there was, CLANG! ... DEBBIE HARRY. I had to stall her for a couple of minutes, which was interesting to say the least. When they were ready, she breezed in, looking amazing. The door went again. I took up my new vocation as door opener to see, CLANG! ... TINA

WEYMOUTH & CHRIS FRANTZ, from TALKING HEADS. One of the greatest rhythm sections ever. I invited them in and pinched myself.

This heavyweight showbiz gathering was nothing compared to when we played in Los Angeles. After an incredible show, we were whisked to The Viper Rooms to meet our guests. Brace yourself clang fans. Within an hour I had met, CLANG! ... GWEN STEFANI, CLANG! ... GAVIN ROSSDALE, CLANG! ... ROBBIE COLTRANE, CLANG! ... LEONARDO DiCAPRIO, CLANG! ... MATT SORUM & DUFF MCKAGEN, from GUNS & ROSES, and, CLANG! ... CERYS MATTHEWS, who was now travelling with us as she was dating Ant. The Viper room was very dark, and so, after a while, and an overdose of clanging, I slipped out and went and sat outside the bar next door.

I ordered a drink and sat back, once again pinching myself at who I had just met, and that they had all commented on how much they had enjoyed the show. A lady passed me and asked if I was alone. She then sat and we started chatting. I have no recollection of her name or what she did etc, but after I asked about all things Hollywood, the sign, the hills and Mullholland Drive etc, she offered to drive me up and show me. So that's what we did. It was amazing. We drove through all the famous roads and she pointed out the relevant showbiz homes. It was fascinating. I got back just as everyone was getting on the bus. I got out of the very expensive looking Mercedes, and thanked the very expensive looking driver for the tour. There was a hush when I got on the bus. Some people just don't believe a good tour guide story.

On one long overnight journey, I was on Strummer watch. All the band and crew were still up partying, so Joe and I found a quiet corner at the front. 'You know you've got it right kid', he said. 'The balance. Don't ever change.' I knew what he meant, and I never forgot that moment, well I did about two hours and half a bottle of brandy later, but that memory is clear today, unlike the morning after. Damn you Strummer watch. After one show, in the middle of nowhere, Joe decided he wanted to escape and grabbed me and Tim and threw us in a taxi. We found an old red neck bar in the middle of nowhere. They had no idea who Joe was, and he played up to it brilliantly. Everyone he got chatting to got a different story of these three cats strolling through town. We were trainee astronauts, chemical scientists, and undercover secret agents. The list went on and on until we had run out of stories. At the end of the night everyone in the bar stood for a photo, which probably still hangs on that wall, wherever it is. Just your average five-legged Space detectives, on a mission from God.

The drug side of the American adventure was quite entertaining if you weren't participating. I would watch as the boys would roll into town and go off and score their stuff. There were a few scary stories of dicey moments with the wrong kind of people, and some hilarious ones. My favourite memory was of them jumping back onto the bus, proud as punch at their purchase. As the bus moved off, they opened up their little package and, one by one, put their nose in, not for a hit, but for a general whiff. 'it's shit' said Pablo. 'It bloody well is' agreed Scott. Now me being not so well versed on all things druggy, I just assumed that this was a term for their purchase. I enquired 'Is that a good thing?' 'No Smiley' they all simultaneously shouted in reply. 'It's actual shit'. Yes, those bozos had spent their hard-earned wages on a wrap of, shall we say, excrement. Lesson learned. For them and for me. 'Shit not good'.

One rainy night, our bus pulled into a truck stop along side another, far plusher bus. 'Smiley, go see who's on board' instructed Lord Strummer. I went out and knocked on the door. I was invited in. They had a white carpet and asked me to take off my shoes. I introduced myself and then realised that, CLANG! ... CHRIS CORNELL, was sitting on the sofa. When I told him who was on our bus, he asked to come back with me. Let's just say he didn't have to take his shoes off.

When we were playing in Chicago, I realised The Who were too. I called Zak and went to his hotel late afternoon for a catch up. We were playing a late show that evening, so I was in no rush to get back. The hours flew by and the phone rang. It was time for Zak to walk down and meet the bus to his show, in a significantly bigger venue than ours. We went down in the lift and once on the ground floor, walked down a long corridor towards reception. As we were walking, we were suddenly joined by people who seemed to come from nowhere. Zak started introducing me. 'This is Smiley, he's playing tonight at The Metro with Strummer'. He introduced me to the crew, the tour manager, and then, to CLANG! ... ROGER DALTREY, CLANG! ... PETE TOWNSEND, and, CLANG! ... JOHN ENTWHISTLE. We all walked through reception and they all said goodbye, sent their regards to Joe and were driven off. That my friends, is what you call, a moment.

My air miles were in full flow when we flew out to Australia, via Japan and New Zealand, to appear at the, month long, Big Day Out festival. When we arrived in Auckland the band turned left, and I turned right, and headed straight to Aussie Mick's house. What a joy to see my best friend, with someone else paying the air fare. We hung out for a couple of days before heading to the first show together. The line up was amazing, once again with all the bands staying in the same hotels. CLANG! ... THE RED HOT CHILI PEPPERS, THE FOO FIGHTERS, BLINK 182, PRIMAL SCREAM, NINE INCH NAILS, as well as, CLANG! ... SARAH COX, and, CLANG! ... GOLDIE. Everyone on the travelling festival, which moved across the great down under to appear at each of the major cities.

It was nicknamed the big day off, as there were four or five day gaps between shows. Most of the bands slotted club gigs in the gaps. We played club shows in Sydney and Melbourne. Mick came to Sydney, and we hung out for five days, playing backgammon and going to see some of the other bands play shows. We went to see the Chili Peppers at the Sydney entertainment centre. Amazing gig, we sauntered backstage to see our new friends. The big burly bouncer showed us through, to the alley behind the venue. Wrong passes apparently. We laughed, and went back and played more backgammon. At one of the festival shows, I was standing outside the dressing room when a strange looking man came up for a chat. He looked like Foo Man Choo, with his long moustache and strange outfit. Nice chap, American accent. After hugging Strummer and I, before heading off into the Sydney festival site, Joe looked at me and smiled. 'You've no idea who that was have you kid?' Turns out it was, CLANG! ... ANTHONY KIEDIS. Fooled me, and sixty thousand festival goers evidently, as he strolled around the festival in his disguise without being recognised, apart from by the Foo Man Choo fans.

We had a show booked at a club called the Sydney Metro. It was Mick's last day, so it was going to be a special evening. Now if you're a drummer there's probably nothing more off putting, five minutes before a show, than being told who was in the crowd. DRUMMER CLANG! ... CHAD SMITH (Chili Peppers), DAVE GROHL & TAYLOR HAWKINS (Foo Fighters), and, DARRIN MOONEY (Primal Scream). Despite my sudden realisation that some of the worlds best drummers were in the room, it turned out to be a great night. Possibly my favourite ever Strummer show, finishing with a Chili Pepper hug between encores. Could it get any better? The next day I said goodbye to my friend from down under and headed to the roof to sit by the pool and take in a bit of Oz vitamin D. I was all alone until I heard the words 'Great show last night, mind if I join you'. No one says no to, CLANG! ... DAVE GROHL, do they? Absolutely the nicest man and best drummer on the planet. This tour couldn't get any more surreal could it? Oh yes.

After our performance in Adelaide, Joe pulled me aside. He had his wife and eight-year-old daughter with him. 'Smiley, would you take Eliza (his daughter) up to see the Chili Peppers later?' Of course I agreed. 'You'll be met at the side of stage just before nine. I've sorted it.' So, at five to nine me, and eight-year-old Strummer junior, stood patiently side of stage, when we saw the band and entourage walking towards us. They all smiled at us as they climbed the stairs up towards the stage. CLANG! ... FLEA, was last. He grabbed Eliza's hand. She grabbed mine. Then to the screams of sixty-thousand fans,

Anthony, Chad, John, Flea, Eliza and Smiley, took to the stage. We were led across by Flea to the far side, and parked to the right of his bass amp. We watched the whole show from there. The surreal scale was now wobbling. At a party the following evening I got chatting to a lovely bubbly Aussie girl. She was a singer songwriter and I remember her name was Sia. Years later I was doing a charity show and one of the guest singers who stood in front of my drums was, CLANG! ... SIA. Now one of the biggest star's in the world, but still the same bubbly Aussie.

Another personality to brighten your day was, CLANG! ... MANI. The mischievous Mani. He was one of life's funny men. A hero to all music fans with The Stone Roses and, now, bass player with Primal Scream. Also, a massive practical joker. During our set I had to switch instruments. Pablo would get behind the kit, Scott would move to guitar and I would play bass. I decided the best and coolest way to do this was to sit on the front of the drum riser as Scott wore his bass so low I couldn't see the strings. This was OK until the second time we performed the track and, looking down and concentrating on hitting the right notes, I kept feeling sharp pains in the side of my head. This went on until I looked across to see Mani, with a bag of jelly babies, aiming them at my head. He thought it was hilarious. Everybody did. Sadly for me, this only spurred him on to bigger and better missiles, culminating in our last show in Perth and two full fruit bowls being directed to my newly shaven napper. Let me tell you friends, bananas, tangerines and specifically pears thrown from twenty yards away, hurt, a lot. Especially if it is all of your five a day.

## CHAPTER 22
## ... KEITH MOON FOR 2 MINUTES

We were invited to the Notting Hill Arts Club for a band meeting. When I got there, Joe was with his wife Luce, and, CLANG! ... COURTNEY LOVE. I'm not usually intimidated by women, but at that point of kissing her rock star cheeks, I felt like I was an eight-year-old at school sports day trying to impress the girls in year three with my athletic prowess before tripping over at the start of the 100 metres. Joe informed us of the upcoming plans. It was time to tick another box on the bucket list. CLANG! ... JOOLS HOLLAND. The man who could turn, 'Do they know it's Christmas', into a boogie woogie pub singalong; whose BBC2 show was the live music show every musician wanted to be on. It was filmed at the now redundant, and probably bulldozed, but still iconic, BBC TV Centre. I used to love it there, you would see all sorts of people mooching between studios. I've shared lifts with all the greats. The legend that is, CLANG! ... GARY LINEKER, the lovely, CLANG! ... GRAHAM NORTON, and, in my opinion, the not so lovely, CLANG! ... JIM DAVIDSON. The BBC lift was the place to hang out if you wanted to stalk the cream of BBC light entertainment.

We arrived for our camera rehearsals mid-afternoon. There is always a big buzz when you do these live shows. The excitement, combined with nerves, that a live show brings. It was like You Bet all over again, just a bit cooler and, hopefully, more mature, but with less hair. Another exciting prospect is always to see who else will be on the show. Could be anyone. David Bowie, Led Zeppelin, The Stones. We had Tracey Chapman, banging on about how fast her car was, Warren Zevon singing about Werewolves in London, and an African band whose bass player's bass lit up. Not quite as staggering as I had imagined. We ran through London Calling, and Jools lent in and said 'Good drumming'; I'll take that. Imagine if we'd done it in the boogie-woogie style? We did two more new tracks before deciding to do 'I Fought The Law', with guest piano player, of course, dear Jools. Joe decided to tell him the wrong key, to trip him up, but he still played it right. Say what you will about him, he knows how to tickle an ivory.

Nobody even noticed a small, but significant, detail, when the show was aired the following day. Joe Strummer and The Mescaleros opened the show, pouring with sweat and looking pretty drained. Ten minutes later they popped up to do their second number, dry as a bone, and fresh faced. You see, after the show had finished it was pointed out that there was a bit of a clanger in our, show opening, version of London Calling, so they made us do it again at the end, with the also sweating and, by now, pretty exhausted crowd (having had to sit through Fast Car for the third time; Tracey isn't the biggest laugh; and matey's lighting bass trick had worn thin within eight seconds). Everyone pretended it was the start of the show, full of beans and enthusiasm, and sweat.

It was around this time that Joe was writing and preparing for his next album. It was taking a different path from its predecessor, a more folky sound. Through the grapevine came three offers. One to support, CLANG! ... PEARL JAM. That was turned down because it apparently wasn't cool. Then, a VH1 show was offered as an option, with, CLANG! ... BRUCE SPRINGSTEEN. Imagine my utter open-mouthed reaction when I heard we had turned that one down as well. When offer number three came in, even Joe couldn't say no. To support, CLANG! ... THE WHO, on their UK Arena tour. I suppose one out of three isn't bad. So, we rehearsed up our forty-five-minute set. It was, rather reluctantly on Joe's part, a balance of old favourites, yet to be released works in progress, and some heavily disguised punk classics now done in a folk style including the new and, not many would agree, improved, Folk Riot. That would confuse the people coming in, trying to find their seat in the darkened arena. You see as super glamourous as it sounds, arena supports can be somewhat heart sinking. No one really hears your first four songs, they realise there is a support band on during the fifth, get settled and then confused by the choice of songs six and seven, and realise who is on stage as you're finishing the last song. Then you're done for the night, by about a quarter past eight.

The boys used to just get hammered. I on the other hand, would sit side of stage every night, watching the greatest rock band in music history, with my mate Zak playing drums. It was amazing. After about the fourth show the monitor man gave me my own set of in ear monitors, and a chair, so that I could listen to what Zak was hearing. What a dream gig that was. What happened next (and, if you've been paying attention, not for the first time), was one of those schoolboy dreams we all have. The one where you're at Wembley, watching England play Germany in the World Cup Final, when the England striker is injured and stretchered off. The man on the tannoy says, 'Due to injuries England don't have any substitutes today. Is there anyone here who could play up front for the rest of the match?' The ninety-thousand people go quiet as I put my hand in the air. 'You, the good-looking chap at the back' (Might have embellished that bit). Then, after quickly putting on my England kit, I go on and score a hat-trick, and England win the World Cup. You know, that dream?

Well, at Sheffield Arena on a rainy Thursday evening, that dream nearly became reality. Only difference was this dream didn't involve shin pads. We had played our set and as we sat back in the dressing room, there was a knock on the door. 'Is your drummer there?' a man with a walkie talkie asked. I went out to greet him. 'How many Who songs do you know?' he urgently enquired. 'All of them' I confidently bullshitted, as a reply. 'Right, well Zak has missed his flight, so you might have to play drums tonight.' The world stopped spinning. All around me people stopped moving. Clouds stopped moving across the sky, and there was a hush across planet Earth, because, at that precise moment, I WAS IN THE WHO!!! 'I'll be back in a minute to get you, then you need to come and see Pete.' That'll be, CLANG! ... PETE TOWNSEND, technically my new boss. I took a massive deep breath and went back into the dressing room. 'Everything Ok kid?' asked Joe. 'Yeah, just off to drum for the Who'. There was another knock at the door. As I opened it, I saw Zak being whisked across the backstage area towards his dressing room flanked by men talking into their wrists. I had been in The Who for precisely two minutes. Now, does that make the CV?

As I said before, Joe had a strange band of merry men in his entourage. One strange cat was called Pockets. He seemed to be everywhere, and was a complete fruitloop. He was standing with, CLANG! ... KATE MOSS, at one of our shows, and I jokingly said to her 'Let me know if he's annoying you.' She's a feisty one old Kate, and she put me firmly in my place.

And then there was a menacing journey on a tour bus from Manchester to Scotland. A few of, what we will refer to as the 'tastier' pals of Joe, along with a few assorted hardcore Mancs, CLANG! ... BEZ, and, CLANG! ... ROWETTA, both from the Happy Mondays, were on board. It was carnage. I went and hid in my bunk. The next day, when I went downstairs to get a cup, I looked out at the Glasgow skyline (raining obviously). I saw Strummer walking around the bus with a placard. Apparently, we were getting kicked off the bus because of the previous evening's shenanigans, and he was performing a one-man demonstration. 'Bit harsh chucking us off' I thought, then I found out that the tour manager had had a knife pulled on him, and the driver had been threatened into a dramatic late night McDonalds stop, fifty miles out of his way. After Joe's admirable one-man stance, we collected our bags and the driver raced off at high speed. Stranded in Glasgow (still raining), we did the gig, and then had to get an overnight train back to London.

Joe had given production duties on his new album to Martin and Scott. The last I saw of Joe was in the toilet at Wembley Arena, after the final Who show, and he told me he wanted me in the studio to record the drums. He would be in touch. A few weeks later I had heard nothing. Then my pal Tony Mullins, popped in for a cuppa. Mullins was a legend in the industry. He used to store and deliver equipment. I went to his lock up in Windsor once, on a mushroom farm. He had four massive aircraft hanger types of buildings full of flight cases. One was chock full of Oasis' gear alone. He also had Take That's, Kylie's and Craaaaaiiig David's. Everyone knew Tone. He's also famous for the best one liner ever, if it is indeed true.

He claims he was standing at a cubicle backstage somewhere, when, CLANG! ... BONO, was standing on his left. Suddendly, CLANG! ... THE EDGE, was standing on his right. As they were all doing what boys do standing up in toilets it is alleged that he said the now immortal words 'Look at U2, Look at Us 3.' Genius.

Anyway, halfway through his PG Tips in my kitchen, he told me how he'd been in the studio with Joe the day before, and how good my drums were sounding. Now it didn't take a rocket scientist to work out the next bit. Martin and Scott were both multi instrumentalists. Scott was the former drummer with Gun. They were given a chunk of money to produce the new album and, rather than pay the band to play their parts, they did it themselves. Now I didn't blame them at all. Given the situation, I may have done the same myself. Suddenly I wasn't sure where I stood. I was due to be playing in Willesden with a covers band on the upcoming Saturday. I sent a message to Joe telling him and he said to pop in. I was in two minds whether to or not. Would it be awkward with Scott's drums on the tracks? If I didn't go in would they take it as a snub? Circumstance took control of the situation, or as it’s also known, my best mate Si, who was driving. Due to traffic, we got to our gig very late and by the time we had finished and were ready to leave it was gone 2am. As hardcore as they all were, I didn't think anyone would be at the studio at that time on a Saturday night, so I went home. Two more weeks went by and I had heard nothing. I phoned Martin. 'Has Joe not called you?' he asked. I was getting the picture. I called Scott. 'Has Joe not called you?' I knew what was coming and twenty minutes later, when Strummer did finally call, we both knew my time was up with The Mescaleros. There was no real reason. Sometimes in music a new face is needed. I actually felt relieved. I'd had a good two year run and was ready for another adventure. I went to see Joe and the boys at Brixton Academy a little while later. It was pleasantries all round.

A few years later I was in my kitchen one rainy morning when Anthony Davie called me. 'Joe's Dead' he said, his voice cracking with emotion. I put the phone down and put Radio London on. I still don't know why I put on that radio station, I never used to listen to it. I seem to recall it was Joe's favourite. The DJ, Robert Elms, was talking about the breaking story which was shocking music fans tuning in around the world. 'If anyone has any stories about the great man, please call in.' I called the number. When I explained who I was they put me straight on air and asked me about my time with the great man. I can't remember to this day what I said, but I do remember the final quote. I said 'I always thought he was Captain Scarlet. Indestructible.' Anthony later told me he had been listening in the car with his family and they had all cried. The funeral was a real star-studded affair, all the people I've mentioned in the past few chapters were there to pay their respects. There aren't many true legends in musical history. Joe Strummer was one of them. R.I.P my friend.

## Chapter 23
## … 4 WEDDINGS AND A SCHOOL FETE

The constant throughout the 90's, was my extra curricular, non fame based, wage-earners. Welcome to the world of covers bands, tribute bands, solos, duos, weddings, corporates, deaf discos, and even school fetes. Yep, I played them all. The best compliments I've ever received have been those that say for all the Clanging in my crazy world, I have my feet firmly on the ground. That, my dear friends, is due to the years, and probably thousands of gigs, I did in pubs, clubs, theme parks, universities, wedding venues and as I said, bizarrely, school fetes. I reckon I must have ticked every box in every musical genre across a thirty year period. I get asked a lot by parents of aspiring drummers, 'What advice can you give my Le? He's the best young drummer in Britain.' 'Well Barry, my first bit of advice would be to take that title from around his neck and pop it back in the box. Then I would advise you to get the, so-called, best young drummer in Britain into a covers band, preferably a good one which isn't named after him.'

You see, when I first got into playing in pubs in my early twenties, I quickly learned that there were some awesome players, and some shockingly shit ones too. A lot of them were playing in pubs for a reason. That was their calling, because they were also the warehouse manager at Costco and, really, playing in the Dog and Fireside on a Friday night, was as far as their musical career was going to take them. Others were destined for bigger and better things, musically I mean, not in warehousing terms. So, after I found my feet in my early covers bands, I worked out how to play the game. I would play each song in the style of the drummer who did it originally. I would play like Ringo on Beatles songs, Charlie on Stones songs, Keith on Who songs, and John on Zeppelin songs. Then, put all those attributes together, and create my own drumming style. So, I was out pretty much five nights a week in different bands doing different stuff. I learnt in pubs that the most important person was the landlord/lady. If you got them in your back pocket you could get work in all sorts of genres.

After a few years, I had learnt to play guitar and sing, to a level that could hold a tune and an audience. So I would suggest to the, now super friendly, landlord/lady that their quiet Tuesday evenings would be a brighter place with yours truly sitting with an acoustic guitar, singing lovely songs that made people feel nice. Also, bringing them in to drink beer and push up their takings. What was not to like? Over the decade, I honed my craft to a point where I was part pub singer, and part stand up comedian. Most people thought I was funny. Some didn't, but as I reminded them, I had a microphone, so I was far more powerful in the put down department than them. So, we covered every base. Solo, duo, trio, four piece, five piece, ten piece with brass section. It was all there.

I hit the jackpot in the 2000's, when I put together a three piece called Smileys Heroes. I spent a month quietly going to pubs and watching the other bands on the circuit. I made notes of what worked and, more importantly, what didn't. I noticed how laboured the bands were. There was no humour. Heads down, playing the same old songs. Forty-five minutes bang on, they would announce their break, and come back half-an-hour later for another forty-five minutes, probably ending with Freebird, and then disappearing into the night. It needed shaking up. I decided to front it using my legendary guitar skills (said no one ever). I do have a brilliant right hand. I put my old mate Simon, now a fully fledged headmaster, on drums, and then grabbed Treasure, my bass playing pal from years gone by, to complete the trio. We came up with a plan which consisted of in ear monitors, which no one else at the time had, by which we could be subtle and talk to each other during songs. The idea was not to stop, to announce the next song while still playing. No gaps, no golf claps. We started trying it out and It seemed to work quite well. We were playing various pubs in the area and it all seemed to be going smoothly. We needed a challenge.

As I was driving home one Friday evening from a rehearsal in London, I passed through Hampton Court. Right next to the building where I was born was a pub called the Cardinal Wolsey. I slowed down to see a band playing. I went in and realised this was where we could really test ourselves. I found the landlady and introduced myself. 'I've heard of you, you were the one who played with Robbie.' she said. Yes, I was and, yes, I was going to use Robbie to get my foot in the door. So, after a little chat she booked us in for an upcoming Friday night. When the night arrived and we were set and ready to go, I told Si and Treas to make sure they had had a wee before we started. They looked at me as I smiled. 'Brace yourselves.' I said after the wee's were taken, and we took to the stage. 'Good evening everyone, we are Smileys Heroes and this is what should be happening here every Friday night'. Two hours and fifty-five minutes later, I said 'thank you and goodnight'. We hadn't stopped, even for a pause between songs. Si and Treas looked at me like they wanted to punch me. 'Don't be shortchanged next time a band stop after forty-five minutes. Goodnight'. I had people from other bands cursing me for months after that. It was a bit of a one off, a challenge which was achieved.

We then branched out into the wedding market. Same approach, same songs. All we needed was some suits and, occasionally, Kerry to add a bit of glamour and a proper singing voice. We used to play 'who's got the best shoes.' I used to get emails from brides requesting their first dance. We would learn it, play it, they'd dance, everyone would get drunk and Bob's your live-in lover, job done. Until one evening when a happy couple had requested that old Van Morrison favourite, 'Brown Eyed Girl'. We had murdered it hundreds of times in the pub's so no need for any extra curricular for this particular do. When we arrived the eager bride and groom came straight over to ensure we had learnt their special song. After I reassured them of our professionality in this field, they reminded me of the alternative version they had sent for learning, the one to accompany their seven weeks of dancing lessons for their precious moment. Uh oh. What could possibly go wrong? I later learnt that they had sent me a version which included a whole salsa style middle section, which these two Strictly fans had spent countless hours, and a lot of money on dance lessons, perfecting to the finest of precisions that would make Tess Daley dribble. The hours of detail they had put into this one special moment were only undone by a band looking lost, like a small child in Toys R Us; or like Torville and Dean, upon realising the ice had melted. It was a disaster. Let's put it this way, it was a very long night for no money.

Another wedding, I was dared to try and catch the bouquet thrown by the bride towards her baying bridesmaids. I was pretty bored and I love a challenge so as she stood on the steps, with half a dozen pink singletons dying to get their hands on the precious 'you're next in the wedding stakes' flowers, I stood just behind, slightly to the left and, as she was right handed, cunningly figuring her trajectory would be at a forty-five degree angle. Also, she had a pro-wrestler-like frame, so I calculated she might get some pretty good flight out of the chrysanthenum/tulip combo. Sure enough, the Bride launched the flowers like they were on an Apollo mission, and they sailed way over the brides-to-be and into my hands, like Ben Stokes at first slip. I should have quietly smiled at Treasure and Si for completing my challenge. I realise now that running around the wedding grounds with my hands in the air like Alan Shearer scoring at Wembley was probably, with hindsight, a bit of a misjudgement on my part, so I would like to take this opportunity to apologise to the six women dressed in pink baying for my blood.

While I am at it, it's probably worth apologising to everyone at the wedding where we were also supplying the incidental music between our sets. This was twenty years ago, way before Ipods and even the Discman, so Si in all his practical helpfulness brought his lounge hi-fi unit, much to his wife's annoyance. His ex-wife actually. Coincidence? Who knows? Anyway, it was one of those old versions that took six CD's and played them on shuffle. I popped what I thought were relevant wedding fodder into the Toshiba and we went off to raid the buffet. Now have you ever listened to Fatboy Slim's first album 'You've Come A Long Way Baby'. It's a brilliant album. Rockafeller Skank; Right Here Right Now;

Praise You; great tunes to wolf down sausage rolls to, before having to go back on stage and murder more Beatles songs. The only slight oversight was that track three on the Fatboy album was called 'F*****g In Heaven', which repeats the non-wedding-friendly F word at least fifty times, just about the same time it takes to drop your cheese and pineapple, and break the world hundred metres sprint record across the dancefloor to smash the off button, and, as it turns out, the play button, pause button, and, basically, every other button on Si's home hi-fi. As I say, any coincidence in the marriage scenario? I'll let you decide.

We had started using agents too, who came up with all sorts of bonkers gigs. We played Butlins and were introduced from behind a curtain. As we kicked in with a Beatles tune, the curtains opened and there was a sea of seven-year-olds, trying desperately to dance to 'Ticket To Ride'. It was quickly changed to a Beyonce tune. Another one was a gig at Reading University. As we powered along, everyone was dancing, in a slightly strange, out of time, way, and making bizarre hand gestures to one another. The agent had failed to point out that we were playing the deaf society annual Christmas ball.

The same agent once got me a Christmas Eve solo gig. I was told to be ready to start at seven thirty and would have to play three one-hour sets. As it was Chrimbo, I asked if there was anything special or unusual about the gig. 'Just your normal, run of the mill show' was his answer. What he failed to point out was the fact that there wasn't a single person under the age of seventy, at least three quarters of them were in wheelchairs, and none of them liked Oasis songs. I managed to limp through the hundred and eighty minutes of hell before going home to cry. The agent called me three days later to say they had had a complaint from several of the oap's, claiming they didn't think I had put my heart and soul into the show. I explained the scenario to the agent, made sure the money had cleared, and fired him. Ho ho ho.

Playing in pubs alone, with just an acoustic guitar, toughens you up. Imagine a cold a rainy Tuesday night in Roehampton, playing to five people who are only there because there's nothing good on the telly. I created a little world for myself where I would once again play without stopping. I used to get so bored that I would randomly change words to see if anyone was listening. They weren't. It was like musical yoga. I would disappear into a bit of a trance for ninety minutes, say thank you and be out of the door, a hundred and fifty pounds richer, within ten minutes. It sapped the life out of me, but it meant the kids wore cool trainers and ate occasionally.

I remember being asked to do a duo on a boat for a wedding ceremony once. They basically wanted us to play an acoustic version of Elbow's 'One Day Like This'. I decided to take Kezza with me to add a bit of wedding class and glamour. The boat was leaving Hampton Court at midday and at a quarter-to we were stuck in traffic. We could see the boat on the other side of the bridge, but the traffic just wasn't moving. I suggested Kez run over the bridge and hold the boat. After a brief discussion about running in six-inch heels, I was powering across the bridge waving my arms at the, about to set off, skipper. After a brief delay, my high-heeled wife turned up in the car and the PA was loaded on. As I say, the brief was basically to play a few chilled-out tunes till it was time for the bride to make the journey from port to starboard.

After about an hour, we got the signal that the bride was ready, and we started our Elbow cover. Now, to this day, I don't know where the misunderstanding was, but twenty-five minutes later we were on the seventy-fifth verse and there was still no sign of the bride. She finally turned up, and sauntered along the wobbly River Thames waves, somewhere between port and starboard and joined her soon to be hubby. I liked the song before, but after we finally finished the longest version in history, I could never listen to it again, which could be said for countless other 'classics' I murdered over the years.

During our rich run of form playing the pub circuit, a new musical outlet came to light. The Tribute Band. This was taking things to another level. Not only did you have to try and sound like the said tribute, you also had to look like them. Now, within a two-year period, I received the award for most appearances in tribute bands, as well as most ridiculous roles. If I told you I played with tributes to The Stereophonics, Travis, Oasis, Robbie, The Style Council, Gwen Stefani, Luther Vandros, Frank Sinatra and Dean Martin, you would probably just about believe me. If I told you I was Noel in Oasish, and Fran Healey in Travising, that might make you slightly more curious. The even more brilliant irony was that I was still doing big festival shows in between and bumping into the real acts. CLANG! ... KELLY JONES, said he was aware of the Stereotonics, CLANG! ... FRAN HEALEY, thought the whole idea of Travising was hilarious, and even threatened to turn up to a show for a duet. CLANG! ... STEVE WHITE, the drummer with The Style Council said he was flattered when I told him how amazing it had been to play his parts. I remember a chat with the Robbie tribute. He was a lovely chap. I remember him saying, in his

Robbie accent 'Have you learnt Strong?' 'I played drums on the original' was my answer. 'But have you learnt my version?' Fifteen all.

The Frank Sinatra, Dean Martin show was hilarious. I was trained in jazz drumming, but I didn't know any of the songs. I bribed the bass player, who was reading sheet music, to count me in and out. Best twenty quid I'd ever spent. We started with Frank singing and then, twenty minutes in, he introduced his old pal 'Deano'. He was at the bar, slightly pissed, chatting up a lady. 'Hey Deano, you wanna come sing with me?' 'Sure thing Frankie, just let me finish making out with this broad.' Wow, I thought, these two are great. They did a couple of duets and then Deano disappeared. About an hour later the same sketch reappeared. 'Hey Deano, you wanna come help me out here?' Cue Deano, absolutely sloshed at the bar, having worked his way through the whiskey section. He staggered up for a duet of My Way, then fell over. Now that, my friends, is taking the tribute world seriously.

I even did a festival. Ready for it, 'Glastonbudget'. The tribute world's own shindig in a field. It was huge. Thousands watched everyone from U2 to Queen, Pink Floyd to Guns N' Roses. My overriding memories of that experience was watching Slash load his guitar amp into the back of his Peugeot 205 after a rousing version of 'Sweet Child O' Mine', still in full Slash get up, and the Robbie tribute coming back with a bloody nose after a jealous boyfriend twatted him for telling his girlfriend 'she was the one'.

My final act in all things tribute, was playing Noel Gallagher, complete with wig and union jack guitar in Dubai with 'Oasish'. As we got to the end of our set, about to deliver a rousing 'Live Forever', I was busy tuning up. The drum intro started. I kicked my tuner back on but missed the opening chord. A furious Liam, or Paul as he was also known, glared at me, and threw a tambourine at my head. After ducking out of the way, things got a little heated afterwards in the dressing room, as Liam and Noel, both still wearing wigs, went toe to toe in true Gallagher style, offering each other outside for a good old fashion tear up, Liam still speaking in a Mancunian accent, me reminding him he was from Reading. Sadly, from that point, my days as Noel, or anyone else pretending they were on Stars in their eyes, were over. Trust me, I don't look back in anger, only slight embarrassment.

# CHAPTER 24
# … ARCHIVE

I got a call from David Enthoven. 'Dear boy, we have a band who need a drummer. Get yourself to this studio tomorrow for 11am.' Bless Dave, he always thought of me when the opportunity came up. So, in my professional capacity as drums for hire I turned up bang on time. CLANG! … ARCHIVE. I was greeted by a mishmash of friendly characters. The studio was downstairs in a basement building, under a hair dressing salon, on a busy corner in Clapham Junction, and a total pain in the arse to get to. I finally got in and sat down with, who were to be, the most prolific band in my career.

There were three of them; Danny, Darius and Craig, with Pete the producer. Over a cuppa, they told me how they were recording album number three and had signed to IE Music (Tim and Dave) as their management. They tried to explain their style. Pink Floyd meets Massive Attack meets Radiohead. When the drums were set and mic'd, they played me the first of two tracks that needed drums that day. The first track was called 'Again'. It was sixteen minutes long. It was like something from 'The Dark Side Of The Moon'. To this day, I've never been so blown away by a song in the studio. It was epic. I got the drums first take. I knew I was onto something a bit special.

Archive songs are like nothing I had ever encountered. They can be long, intricate, drawn out pieces of crazy art, without the traditional layout of verse, chorus, and middle eight. They are bonkers. They are genius. I also realised that Darius Keeler, the main brains behind Archive, is a musical freak. A genuine genius; ably supported by, the similarly brilliantly talented, Danny Griffiths. Darius can hear things nobody I have ever worked with can. A true one off. Soon after the session, plans were made to promote the upcoming new album. I was the Archive drummer.

One of the first bits of promo we did was a TV show in Paris, presented by former MTV VJ, CLANG! ... RAY COKES. What a top dude he was, a real pioneer to later TV presenters like Chris Evans and Johnny Vaughan. We were to play some of the new tracks live in front of an audience and, as a Brucey bonus, perform a version of The Specials classic 'Gangsters', featuring their singer, the legendary CLANG! ... TERRY HALL. My goodness, he was hard work. You could hardly get a word out of him, but it was still a real pleasure to perform such an iconic track with a genuine legend.

We toured the critically acclaimed album across Europe, and it became clear that Archive were quite a big deal in Europe, but not so much in the UK. Their singer at the time was Craig Walker, a feisty ginger Irishman with a striking voice, who was a lovely fella until his third pint. That was usually when all hell could, and generally did, break loose. By the time the next album had been recorded in Paris, tensions within the band were at crisis point and, after one incident too many, Craig was fired by the management. In his place came Dave Pen. He seemed quite shy; and had long hair which he used to hide behind. He looked a bit like Jesus. He was literally dropped into the band days before we were due to tour the new album 'Noise'. He looked so nervous, but as the tour progressed, he started to gain confidence, and had an amazing stage presence.

At this point a girl singer, Maria Q, was sharing vocal duties. A beautiful Italian, who was stylish, cool and demure, unless, as in the case of Stevie Keys, the Hammond player, you slapped her on the arse. It was like a scene from The Exorcist. Her head turned three hundred and sixty degrees before she shot him a look that said, 'do that again and you'll wake up with a horse's head in your bunk.' He never did it again.

The next album, 'Lights', really took the band up another notch. They had brought in another singer, American Pollard Berrier, to perform with Dave and Maria. He had an incredible, almost angelic, voice. The girls in the audience loved him. So, there were now eight members on stage. We were playing bigger and better venues, including arenas in France. Strangely, we seemed to have a revolving door for bass players, but luckily for me, the absolute cream of UK players. Lee Pomeroy, Carl Holt, Dale Davis, Steve Davis, Jonathan Noyce and Matt Round have all played for the band, both on record, and live. Incredible players, and all wonderful men. You have to love your bass player when you're a drummer.

On guitar was Steve Harris, still, to this day, probably the funniest man I've ever met. He was hilarious, and also had the most bizarre party trick. You see, Harris had one enormous bollock, which he had named 'Beryl'. His party trick was to lift it above his belt line when people were taking photos. Now this was a hilarious gag which always brightened people's day. We decided to extend it into the world of the celebrity. My new role, primarily at festivals, was to seek out a celebrity, ask for a photo with them and my good friend Steve, and, as the photo was about to be taken, Steve would whip Beryl out. The celebrity was generally unaware of the scam, so no one was hurt. So, we went hunting for victims. Number one. CLANG! ... MEL C. Good old Sporty Spice, who was now on her solo career, and being a bit of a rocker. I found her and asked for a pic. She happily obliged. In came Steve, Out came Beryl, Mel was none the wiser. Easy.

Next up. CLANG! ... BANANARAMA. Same tactic, same outcome. Steve was popping Beryl out left right and slightly off centre, in any photo opportunity. We probably got a bit cocky (excuse the pun) and took our eye off the ball (again, excuse the pun). Another festival, and I spotted CLANG! ... SHAGGY. Mr lover lover man. I later found out that Shaggy was an ex US Marine. He was certainly built like a brick shithouse. We asked for a pic. We lined up. The photographer said cheese. Shaggy looked down. 'What the f**k is that?' he shouted, as Beryl looked up, winking. Suffice to say we never got a pic with him, and only just got away with our Beryl's intact.

On one of the tours, our support band was Birdpen. This featured Dave and Mickey from Archive, with Jim, their drummer. They were, and still are, a fantastic band, but it was a lot to pull off, playing for the support and main band every night, whilst Ringo (Jim the drummer's nickname, as he also plays in a Beatles tribute band) went and sold merch. It was a long tour. Towards the end we were playing in Hamburg. I was watching BP from the side of the stage and thought it would be a fun idea to start throwing peanuts at Jim. The first few shots were bang on and he was laughing at my shenanigans. Now, Birdpen played along to backing tracks, which were triggered on a pad just to Jim's left. After about my eighth direct dry roasted hit, I decided to try and get a good lob in and crack him on the top of his head. Mid song, the nut flew majestically skyward but overshot its target. The nut bounced onto the drum pad, which triggered the next song. The band panicked, looking at each other as to what was going on, only to then clasp eyes on the Archive drummer, side of stage, with his hands in a big packet of KP. They carried on like troopers and then came off stage. Dave didn't speak to me for a week.

Over the years there were brilliant moments on the road with Archive. At a huge French festival, we were on before, CLANG! ... KASABIAN. They were really sociable before the show, and Dave and I came off stage and raced across to catch their set. There was a moment where Tom the singer held his hands in the air and said, 'Are you with me?' All fifty-thousand French festival goers simultaneously raised their hands in the air and shouted 'Yes.' I nudged Dave. 'You should do that.' By this point, Dave had ceased being Jesus and was now a bit of a heartthrob, with short hair. Sure enough, at our next show, he shouted to the crowd 'Are you with me?' It had the same impact. A new Dave was born.

We also played a festival in Switzerland and were on straight after, CLANG! ... STING. They had two huge adjoining stages, so we stood and watched him before we went on. The next morning at the hotel, there he was, sitting in his bathrobe, probably after a heavy night of tantric sauce, sitting tucking into his Special K. Well, you don't get many photo opportunities like that, so I waited till he had finished and was reading his book. I walked up and asked if he enjoyed the show. 'Well nobody left.' was his cheeky, Sting answer. I laughed, we selfied, I left. Job done.

At a big indoor festival in Portugal, we had a temporary backline tech. He was a funny old sausage. In the middle of our set we all left the stage, leaving just Maria singing to Darius' piano. It was a very dark stage, and someone pointed out that the light above the piano had been knocked and that Darius was struggling to see his keys. Our super temp swooped straight into action, and before you could say 'the switches all look very similar', he moved up from the left and hit the switch. The wrong switch. The switch on the keyboard which then turned everything off, leaving just Maria singing acapella until he could reboot everything back on. His last gig with us if I remember rightly.

Another memory was in a very posh Athens hotel, when our very well-spoken and smartly dressed tour manager had a couple of gin and tonics too many and decided to jump, completely naked, into a fountain. We still don't know why, because after all seeing him naked, it was definitely not the wisest move. There wasn't much of his dignity that needed covering shall we say. Tour managers are a strange breed. Some wonderful, some not. I've had the full bagful over the last twenty-five years. The legend, the liar, the lesbian, the thief, the blagger, the one unknown, who even to the management didn't know was doing it as he was a dep, the moody one, the bonkers one and luckily for me and Archive at this present time, a superstar one.

Our current answerer of every stupid, lazy arsed, question, fired at him by dumb musicians, is Chris Walker. He has the patience of a saint, and also, realising musicians can't tie their own shoelaces without asking him how, is one step ahead of everyone. When we wake up on the tour bus, the first thing we see on our phone is a video of how to get into the venue. This is supplemented by huge signs with the words, 'everything this way'. He is amazing. He also has a quirky pastime, which involves tattooing himself, usually on a moving tour bus. This all seems to go to plan unless he's a bit pissed and decides to tattoo a very wonky smiley face on the back of a technician's knee. Poor old Tim, he of the wonky back of the knee tat.

We were travelling in a big purple tour bus. It was ace. Plenty of room. A massive back lounge with a huge telly where we would sit on long journeys and watch terrible films. If anyone hasn't seen 'The human centipede' I'd swerve it if I were you. The only downside to the purple peril was that it broke down. A lot. Most tours would include the ritual of breaking down in the middle of nowhere, sitting around for hours waiting for a replacement bus before transferring all our gear on to the new bus, realising the new bus was miles better than ours anyway, and then getting to a venue to be greeted hours later by our newly fixed old bus, and having to transfer everything back across, while bemoaning how much better the other one was. It was a pattern that happened many a time.

With the bus came, over the years, a plethora of bus drivers. Wrong way Ron, the grumpy but loveable old man from Leeds, Geordie Colin, a hilarious chap from Newcastle, whose catch phrase was, 'I'm off to my bunk, for a tug'. Say it in a Geordie accent. It's much funnier. We also had Irish Eamonn, and Stinky Barry, who no one knew anything about because you couldn't get near enough to ask him. We got caught up at Calais once in a strike by the ferry company. Irish Eamonn went to make enquiries and came back to say we could be stuck there for four days. He then checked his emergency stash of pot noodles and realised we didn't have enough for four days and fifteen people. He then managed to swerve a purple tour bus out of a queue of parked cars and drove off at high speed to Amsterdam. Legend.

The gigs were getting bigger and so were the bands on the bills with us. We supported, CLANG! ... MUSE, as well as, CLANG! ... BIFFY CLYRO, at the Stade de France in Paris. We were on the same bill as, CLANG! ... 30 SECONDS TO MARS, in Germany, where we watched, side of stage. When they invited audience members up to join them onstage, I couldn't resist. That footage exists somewhere. I'd had a few. Dave and I then set off on a mission to meet, CLANG! ... JARED LETO. I was his wing man. We finally got through all his bodyguards with an AAA pass and a request for a photo for Dave's wife, and he finally came out to greet us. He was tiny and had the limpest handshake of any man I've ever met.

Another memorable festival story was in Germany. We had played late afternoon and were mooching around backstage. I was talking to, CLANG! ... MATT BELLAMY from Muse. Around us was a lot of scuttling, and people talking into walkie talkies. As we looked out from the dressing rooms towards the main stage a storm was heading towards us. It was huge. Suddenly every tour manager rounded up their band members and rushed toward their respective tour buses. Muse's performance was instantly cancelled and, as the storm hit, everybody waded through knee high flood water toward their buses. Our bus slinked its way out of the field, allegedly, fourth in the queue.

We later heard that the fifth bus slid down a burst riverbank and stranded everyone there for days. Good old wrong way Ron was our hero.

The biggest celebrity we all encountered at a festival was undoubtedly, CLANG! ... JACK BLACK. He was performing with his band Tenacious D. It's usually quite reserved backstage at a festival, with musicians occasionally asking for a photo but, mostly, respecting their fellow performers solace in the backstage area. Not on that day. On that day, every musician from every band queued up for a picture. He was, and still is, Hollywood royalty. Ironically, we all have the same picture.

It was always a strange existence being in Archive. You found yourself using the same phrase whenever anyone asked about the band. 'Huge in Europe, couldn't get arrested in the UK'. A good example was when we toured in Europe and our support bands were, CLANG! ... THE ZUTONS, and, CLANG! ... THE KOOKS. What was crazy about that bill was that, at that time, both of those bands were in the top five of the album chart back in the UK. I remember watching The Zutons when they performed a 'new' track called 'Valerie'. I was having a beer with their singer Dave after the show and commented what an amazing song that was. Dale Davis was our bass player at the time, and he went on to play with, CLANG! ... AMY WINEHOUSE. If you ever ask him about the crossover of the worldwide Zutons/Amy 'Valerie' smash hit, he will take full credit. Well he is an Arsenal fan.

Once, on a long tour, we had two days off. This was always a dangerous scenario because it usually meant everyone went a bit nuts. Archive used to love doing DJ sets in random bars on tour, and three or four of the band would take it in turn to drop their block rocking beats. On this particular day, we were all lined up to do a turn from about 9pm. So, at lunchtime we all went to the pub. A few shandies into our afternoon somebody introduced some green herbal concoction. 'If it was herbal it had to be good for you' we convinced ourselves, and all tucked into a pint of green gooey herbal goodness. Nothing really happened and we carried on in the pub until early evening, when it was time to go and DJ. We went back to the hotel to freshen up, ready to meet downstairs at eight.

Now, the herbal green monster was slowly taking effect on everyone but, hilariously, in different ways. It was reported the next day that one member sat for four hours crying on the phone to his Mum, one sat comatose in the corner of the bar, one clung onto the sink all night, and one took over everyone else's DJ duties and was still going strong at seven the next morning. The other funny hallucinatory story was the one backstage at the Paris stadium show. There were several grams of mind enhancing powder wrapped in cigarette papers floating around. That was the popular way of taking it, washed down with water. A member asked another member to put a little bit in paper for him to take. There was a slight misunderstanding, and a whole gram was accidently washed down in one gulp. Five hours later that member was still loving the lights and dancing to the music, three hours after the show had finished.

We were never hedonistic, but learned our lesson in Paris after a live TV show, on a promo tour years later when, after a couple of strong backstage freebie french beers, Mickey and I challenged Dave and Yanos, the six foot five monitor man, to a midnight piggy back race through the rainy streets of Paris. Apart from Mickey breaking his arm after I had dropped him, (that nearly led to him missing the whole tour. God bless the NHS) I felt the race had gone really well.

France has always been Archive's biggest market, and a highlight in the band's career was to headline Sunday night at the Rock en Seine festival, the French equivalent of Glastonbury, complete with a sixty-four piece orchestra, playing to fifty-five thousand people. The power of sitting behind this incredible band and in front of an orchestra is still a monumentous memory and worthy of a look on Youtube.

Twenty-five years after the band started, they released a 'best of' album, ironically called '25'. The body of work they have released, that I've been lucky enough to be part of, is seriously impressive. I've had the pleasure of playing on the albums; You All Look The Same To Me, Michel Vallient, Noise, Lights, Live At The Zenith, Controlling Crowds, Controlling Crowds part IV, With Us Until You're Dead, Axiom, Restriction, The False Foundation and 25. The musicality and pure genius that is Archive is the reason they are still going strong today, the family ethic within the group typified by Holly Martin, our lovely Aussie singer, bringing her ten-month-old son Noah on the 2019 European tour. Obviously, there was a lot of crying, babbling and dribbling, but the baby was really well-behaved.

Archive roll on. Diverse, intelligent, and way ahead of their time. More and more people are now starting to realise just how unique they are, and the band are still selling out across Europe, and even starting to get arrested in the UK. Worth seeing again, and again, again, again, again.

## CHAPTER 25
## ... SUPERGROUPS

I always wanted to be in a supergroup. To my mind I reckon I've been in five. The first was like a boyhood dream. Four Good Men. A Scottish Supergroup. Half Big Country, half Simple Minds. Two of the bands who inspired me as a drummer in my teens, now playing their own songs with original members, CLANG! ... BRUCE WATSON, CLANG! ... MICK McNEIL, and CLANG! ... DEREK FORBES. I couldn't believe my luck. Songs like; Don't You Forget About Me, Alive & Kicking, Fields Of Fire, and In A Big Country. I'd learnt those songs like the back of my hand, from studying Mark Brezecki and Mel Gaynor in my bedroom as a teen. A Scottish drumming dream.

The man in charge was James Newell. Over the years he became one of my bezzies. I used to stay at his flat. He was, actually, the one who reignited my interest in The Alarm; but that's in the next chapter. 4GM started playing predominantly Scottish venues, before venturing over to America and Canada. By this point, they had zoned in on the Scottish angle and acquired two young female bagpipers. Great for the heritage side, a massive pain in the arse when they warmed up in the dressing room. It was like having that woman from the Cranberries singing 'Zombie' every night, in stereo. Our band highlight was supporting, CLANG! ... THE PRETENDERS, in Boston. An immense sold out show. We were invited into their dressing room for a bit of an aftershow. I thought I would have a chat with CLANG! ... CHRISSIE HYNDE. She was having none of it, and had her eyes set on one of the pipers. The drummer was nice though.

Derek and I then went in as rhythm section for a tour with, CLANG! ... SPEAR OF DESTINY. I'd been a big fan of theirs in the late eighties, so it was nice to meet, CLANG! ... KIRK BRANDON. He was lovely, in a slightly whacky way. It was amazing playing their old songs like 'Liberator' and 'Come Back', but tricky getting my head around the dark and moody new album. A couple of pals of mine came to a London show and left after four songs as they felt 'scared'. That sums the experience up quite nicely I think.

Another 'Super' tour was with Bad Co. CLANG! ... MICK RALPHS, was an original member of Bad Company and wrote a lot of the hits, including 'Feel Like Making Love'. To put it into context, I had played that song hundreds of times in pub bands, and I was now sharing a stage with the man who wrote it. The singer was a lovely man called Robert Hart. Devilishly handsome, with amazing hair, which he still owns today. He had one of those rare rock voices, only people like Rod Stewart and Paul Rodgers have. He was also a lively old character. I remember a show we did in Leeds. The intro tape went on, and we strode confidently on stage, crowd cheering. We kicked in with 'Can't Get Enough Of Your Love'. Classic rock. Robert sang the first line and gestured to the monitor man. He in turn kind of shrugged his shoulders and arrogantly sat back in his chair, arms folded. After singing the second line, Rob again gestured for his monitor to be turned up. After the same 'not arsed' response from the monitor man, Rob walked across and punched the guy square in the face, walked back, and carried on as if nothing had happened. I'd never seen anything like it. Suddenly there were three burly looking security guards standing next to the monitor man with the bloody nose. We finished the show and made our way back to the dressing room. The manager came in and locked the door. We then had to hatch a plan to get Rob out of the building, as the three security gorillas were baying for his blood. Nothing like a good old toilet window and fire escape adventure to save the day.

Other 'supers' included, 'Thee Concerned Citizens', made up of Paul Weller's bass player, The Bluetones guitarist and my old mate Greavesie, the Brentford commentator. They recorded a fantastic album but, sadly, only ever played one show. Greavesie introduced me to, CLANG! ... RICHARD ARCHER, from Hard Fi. I'd been quite obsessed with Hard Fi, as I was living in Staines when they became huge. Everyone knew them, or so they claimed. Local heroes. After they had scaled the heady heights of two number one albums, the inevitable third disappointment had led to them falling out of the premier league, never to return. Richard had a studio in Ashford and, after our meeting at Costa in Staines, we started recording together. He once called me at 10pm. He was producing a young band for a record company and was on a strict deadline to deliver the new single by the following morning. He and his right-hand man, ace producer Wolsey White, had been desperately trying to get the track finished but just could not get the young drummer to deliver. So, I was drafted in and at midnight, instructed to play in the style of the young whippersnapper, but more in time, with more feel, and in a way as so no one would know it wasn't him. Trust me, that's harder than it sounds. The case was cracked the next day when the single was delivered and the band, drummer, and record company never spotted the late night cloak and dagger drum sesh.

Rich, Wolsey and I have recently finished a new album with American singer Krysten Cummings and bass ace Dale Davis. The project, 'Offworld', is a stunning album set for delivery in 2020. Watch this space.

Now, as all musicians will testify, gigs don't always go to plan. My darkest day as a musician was when I was drumming for, CLANG! ... REPUBLICA. I had done a show with them at Silverstone Racecourse and all had gone well. They were happy, I was happy. As they would say, 'Baby, I'm Ready To Go'. They had a festival show in Hungary lined up. I was playing the night before in Belgium with Archive. It was agreed I would stay in Belgium overnight and get an early morning flight to Romania. There I would wait for the Republica band and crew, who were flying in from London, to get the connecting flight to Hungary and, boom, a huge festival appearance which would lead to many more. What could possibly go wrong?

I waved goodbye to my Archive chums and got a taxi to my hotel. At six am I was up and showered, and on my way to Brussels airport. I caught my plane to Romania and then read my messages. 'Wait for us in arrivals, we are a couple of hours behind you, then we can get onto the connecting flight together. Love from Saffron.' So, after successfully getting through Romanian passport control, I followed the arrivals signs and plonked myself down in a chair, opposite the incoming passengers and settled down with a good book. Always the best way to kill a couple of hours. I didn't bother checking their arrival time as they were about to walk out in front of me. The clock ticked by. Then my phone rang and it was the tour manager. 'Where the f**k are you?' 'I'm in arrivals waiting for you, where are you?' 'We are on the connecting flight to Hungary, on the runway'. How could this be? There's no way they could have slipped past me, however good my book was. I grabbed my bag and found the departure sign. The plane was indeed leaving. I panicked and raced to the British Airways desk. They informed me that the new Romanian Airport had two Arrivals. They were in the other terminal, or should I say, taking off right above my head. I then found out to my horror that there were no other flights that day to Hungary, and no way of getting there by train or car. I couldn't speak to them for at least two hours as they were on route thirty thousand feet above my head. Meanwhile, the boys from Archive were on their way home on their bus, lovingly enquiring of my status. When I told them they thought it was hilarious. Imagine how funny they found it when I told them the only flight back to the UK that day was to Luton, at 10pm, and was eight hundred pounds. So, two hours later I was called by the tour manager after they had landed in Hungary and had to explain my situation. I then had to ask my wife to get a baby-sitter, and drive to Luton at midnight to collect me. In the meantime, Archive were asking for regular updates, which they found funnier than a re-run of Fawlty Towers. The following days result of Romania's second arrivals terminal was that I was eight hundred quid down, Republica had done the festival with drums on tape and consequently died on their arses and lost future Eastern European festival appearances. My wife got a hundred pound parking ticket from Luton Airport for driving into the wrong entrance. I never heard from, or played with, Republica again. It's still the worst musical day of my life, the only redeeming feature being the Archive boys enjoyed it so much. Buggers.

I got a call from my old Mescalero pal Anthony Davie, asking if I would be up for putting a 'Joe Strummer' tribute act together. He had a show lined up in Italy, and other offers on the table. I put the word out. Original Mescalero Pablo was in with me. Two of the original line up. Throw in former Simple Minds bass player Derek Forbes, and Gary Numan guitarist Steve Harris, and there was your 'Supergroup' right there. All we needed was a 'Strummer'. We put our heads together, but really couldn't come up with a relevant Joe. Then someone suggested we go down the actual tribute route and use someone from a Clash tribute band. Genius. We found one, so memorable I can't even remember his name, and threw a set together, rehearsed it and headed to Italy. Now you might think the man from Tribute World might have felt slightly nervous, surrounded by some pretty heavyweight musical pedigree. Did he f**k. He swanned in like Elton John, demanding this that and the other, and acted like a proper diva. We flew home and Elton was sacked. News of the newly named 'Los Mondo Bongo', a title of one of Joe's tunes, was spreading. Gigs were being offered in the UK and Canada. We needed a frontman. Someone to fill Joe's shoes.

Earlier that year I had been at a festival when I spotted Dave Sharp, former guitarist with The Alarm. We had a lovely chat and he invited me to go into the studio with him and jam some new songs. We chatted about The Alarm and he said Mike was still going strong. Now this was back in the days of Myspace, which looking back, was quite a good way of getting in touch with people you probably couldn't before. One night I cheekily messaged Mike telling him if he ever needed Joe's Drummer (Cheers Noel), I would be well up for it. Incredibly, he replied and asked to meet me in London for an audition. I was early and waited in the room until the door swung open and there he was. We had a chat, then played two songs and went to the pub. The Alarm had a regular drummer at that time called Steve Grantley, so I was basically put on the subs bench in case he tore a hamstring.

The offers for Los Mondo were coming in, and we realised we needed a special frontman, someone who could bring something 'extra' and honour Joe in a unique way. A few names were thrown into the ring, one of them being Mike. I messaged him, asking if he would be interested. He had told me in the pub how much he loved The Clash. Before we knew it, phone calls had been made, Canadian dates confirmed, and we were all at Heathrow terminal five trying to get upgraded. We all tried a different angle. Pablo used his 'Lily Allen producer' card, Derek his 'I was in Simple Minds you know', and my pretty piss poor 'I used to play with Robbie and I've got tonsillitis' effort. We all walked to the plane and turned right, all apart from Mike, who went left to business class. Was it because he was The Alarm frontman, had sold millions of albums worldwide and still looked like a rock star with his impressive blonde mane? No, it was because his mate Dave worked for BA. Life can be so simple when you want it to be.

So, we hit Canada, and then a run of UK dates. I was really enjoying playing behind Mike. He was infectious, and brought every show to life, while truly honouring the spirit of Joe. He immersed himself in the role and the shows were a real success. Now, some cynics amongst you might say I used those shows to audition my way into Alarm world. Well cynics, it was actually fate, and being sat next to Mike at the right time, that determined our future together.

The Alarm were due out on tour when we finished our UK dates, and Mike had Danny Farrant from The Buzzcocks lined up to do the first three shows, as Steve Grantley was away with Stiff Little Fingers, and wanted a week off between tours. Fair enough. Mike and I were sitting in the back lounge of the tour bus when Danny called to say he was now unable to do the three dates as his wife was expecting and she needed him with her. So, as I made the tea Mike rang Steve. When I returned, with two superb cups of PG Tips (I make a mean cup, ask everyone in every band I've ever toured with, as that seems to become my role, bus tea boy. It's not a coincidence, it's a skill), Mike looked unusually agitated as he said, and I quote, 'I'm begging you Steve, it's just for three of the shows and I'm totally stuck for a drummer.' He put down the phone. Steve had refused. 'I wish you weren't away with Archive mate' he said forlornly. This, my friends, is where the seven worlds collided. 'I'm only unavailable for the first three shows. How about I get you a dep for them, and I do the rest of the tour?' It was a done deal. My pal Paul Davis stepped in for the first three, and then it was time for me to board the good ship Alarm.

# CHAPTER 26
# ... THE ALARM IS RINGING

I had been a huge fan of The Alarm in my mid-teens. If you recall from chapter one, I was hanging with my cool older friends and we went to see the band at Hammersmith Palais. This was before Declaration, their first album. I had bought the singles, and we stood amongst the sell out crowd, near the back waiting for the band. Now I recall Mike Peters walking in the back door and us saying hello to him. I remember him being incredibly tall, in a huge leather jacket with massive hair. I was only fourteen and about four-foot-eight. No wonder he seemed so big. Who would have thought that years later me and the tall man with massive hair would be best mates. My voice hadn't even broken at that point, but I do clearly remember I loved that gig. They were immense. It inspired me. I can remember my cousin Paul being a huge fan too. It made me want to be a drummer, and play at The Palais, for a band like The Alarm. Be careful what you wish for kids.

So, when I joined, the band was made up of diverse characters who, shall we say, had been around the musical block. CLANG! ... CRAIG ADAMS, CLANG! ... JAMES STEVENSON, and, CLANG! ... MARK TAYLOR. These three legends had played with everyone from Elton John, to The Mission, to The Cult, to Simple Minds, to Kim Wilde, to The Sisters of Mercy, to Sinead O'Connor. I was once again the youngest by quite a few years, and I lapped up their showbiz stories, and boy did they love my lapping. Nights on the tour bus with these musical troubadours were never dull. It was nearly all over before it began after, what is now recalled as 'The Isle of Wight incident'. It was 2010. We were booked to play the

Isle of Wight festival and Mike and Jules, being the ace boss and Mrs Boss, had decided that, rather than a dodgy old B&B like most bands, we would all stay in a massive house overlooking the sea, partners included. So, I brought Kezza with me for what would be an epic weekend. You see, after we were due to play at lunchtime on Saturday, the rest of the day was pure Gold. First up, Spandau Ballet. This is back in the day before, CLANG! ... STEVE NORMAN, became our lovely friend. Following the eighties New Romantics was the incredible Pink, and then the biggest and best of all, Sir Paul McCartney. What a day it would be.

Our performance in the big top was fab, especially when we were joined onstage by Squeeze legend, CLANG! ... GLENN TILBROOK, for a stomping version of 'Sixty Eight Guns'. The performance was fab and enjoyed by all the band and other halves alike. At three o'clock Kez and I decided to venture off into the throng of the festival, telling everyone we would catch up with them later. At that point the tour manager said something to me, which to this day I realise I didn't quite hear. So, seven hours later, myself and my now gorgeously sozzled Mrs were singing our hearts out to Beatles classics. He finished with Hey Jude and, after a big celebratory hug, we headed back to the bus to go back to our lovely big house. Finding the bus, after using all our free beer tokens, proved slightly trickier than first planned but eventually we spotted it. The lights were on and the engine was running. We walked up to the side and opened the sliding door. As a celebration of the perfect evening I decided to sing, at the top of my drunken voice 'Live and let die' as the door rolled open. There, sitting in front of us, were the whole band and all their other halves, looking mightily cheesed off. Not a word was spoken. Strange. The journey back was made in total silence, the air filled only with dirty looks aimed at my wife and me. The alcohol consumption, especially on her part, seemed to have an 'ah whatever' effect, and the silent bus pulled into the huge driveway. We wished everyone a goodnight and received no reply, other than some more dirty looks and talking under breaths. The next morning, we sat on the veranda with Mike and Jules. They had left the festival earlier than everyone else and were having a sneaky giggle. When I enquired as to what was attributing to their jolly mood, they proceeded to explain the reason for the previous evening's dirty looks. You see, the tour manager's words I had missed had been along the lines of 'We are leaving at nine, don't be late'. It transpires Kez and I rolled up at eleven. They had all been waiting for two hours while we were singing along with Macca. Mike and Jules thought it was hilarious, but apparently my new band mates didn't, and their better halves definitely didn't. Not the best way to introduce yourself into Alarm world but as I say, the boss and Mrs boss loved it so, hey ho.

When the first tour was over Mike asked me to go into the studio with him. I drove to deepest darkest Wales, through the valleys and down into a no internet existence. I didn't arrive till 11pm but Mike seemed keen to set the drums up there and then, ready for the following day's recording. An hour later, with drums set and mic'd, we decided to record new drums on an existing Alarm track. The song was called 'Trafficking'. It's still one of my favourite Alarm songs I've played on, and one of my proudest recordings. I got it in one take and when I walked into the control room Mike threw his arms around me. It was the first of hundreds of recordings we would share together and is still an incredible memory.

Two words I kept hearing during my early Alarm career were 'The Gathering'. I finally asked what this mystical event was, and was told that every January, The Alarm host a weekend in North Wales, called, ironically, 'The Gathering'. A weekend of live performances by The Alarm and other special guests, as well as quizzes, story telling, films, walks, singalongs and lots of alcohol. My first Gath was their twenty first and was being held at the legendary 'Pontins' in Prestatyn. I remember seeing it in the 'On the buses' film in the early seventies. When I arrived I realised not a lot had changed since Reg Varney drove his big red bus to the holiday camp with Jack, Olive and his Mum. The chalets were exactly the same. The joy was that the holiday camp itself was shut to the public, but we were staying there for a week to rehearse before two thousand Alarm fans descended on its hallowed grounds on the Thursday night and drank it dry till it was time to leave on Sunday night.

Famously, every year, there is a coach from Glasgow, and they are all so hammered by the time they arrive, I don't think they've ever seen a Friday night gig. Have you ever stayed at a deserted holiday camp? It's ace. The band and crew had a chalet each, all in a line, so after rehearsing we used to go back to our little holiday homes and meet again the next morning. It sounds dull but it was brilliant. When Thursday evening came and the gates were opened, Alarm fans came pouring into the camp. The bars were full, and the drinking began. The Gathering is still going strong today and over the years have had some fantastic guests including, CLANG! ... SIMON FOWLER (Ocean Colour Scene), CLANG! ... STEVE

NORMAN (Spandau Ballet), CLANG! ... BILLY DUFFY (The Cult), CLANG! ... IAN McNABB (The Icicle Works), and, CLANG! ... GLENN MATLOCK (The Sex Pistols); as well as many others I can't recall. The thing that makes the weekend's so special is the bond between the band and the fans. Everyone is there for the same reason so there is no 'them and us'. It's what makes The Alarm different to any other band I've been involved in. Everyone knows each other and everyone is lovely. People come from all over the world to these special gatherings. It's a fan base built on Love Hope and Strength.

At one Gathering, Mike and I decided to do a duo performance on the Friday evening. 'That's OK' I thought. Him on guitar, me on drums. White stripes. It turns out I was right about Mike's part of the duet. Mine however, consisted of playing drums, and percussion with my feet, whilst strumming a mandolin, and singing into a three part harmonising microphone. That's three out of tune voices if you get it wrong. I felt like a plate spinning clown. On the upside, Auden guitars made me my own mandolin. I must have been good. Luckily, no film of the event exists to prove me right, or more likely, wrong.

Back in the studio, and Craig Adams had flown in from America to record some new tracks with myself and Mike. We set up in the live room to record together. He was jet lagged, slightly pissed and very sleepy. So much so that he sat on a stool to play his bass. We were halfway through a track when suddenly the bass stopped. I looked across and there he was, head back and fast asleep, mid-song. Mike and I burst out laughing. We called it a night and left him there. Eight hours later, when we went back to the studio, he was still in exactly the same position, snoring his little head off. Jet lag and Merlot. A lethal combination.

Recording over the years has taken us in all sorts of directions, with all sorts of people. We recorded the music to a film, 'Vinyl', which starred Quadrophenia and Blur legend, CLANG! ... PHIL DANIELS. It was amazing spending three days in the studio with Phil and Mike, and the stories had me fascinated. I've been lucky enough to record thirteen albums with Mike including; 21, The Sound & The Fury, re-works of, Declaration & Strength, Vinyl, Blood Red Viral Black, Equals, Sigma, Stream, and, The Sun Studio Sessions, as well a live album recorded at The Cardiff Millennium with an orchestra and two choirs.

A memorable evening was spent at BBC Wales when we again performed with a choir and orchestra for a radio special. It was a very significant evening for me personally, as it was the first time I got to meet my dear friend Alan Thompson. Big Al was the compere for the evening and a DJ for BBC Radio Wales. We instantly became firm friends and in years to come I was a guest on his show on numerous occasions. Once we did an interview with me at a BBC studio in London and him in Cardiff. I was shown through to an empty waiting room. Five minutes later, in walked, CLANG! ... SIMON DAY, from The Fast Show. We sat opposite each other but said nothing. After the interview, as I was leaving, he came out too. I plucked up the courage to tell him I'd been dying to say 'someone’s sitting there mate', one of his brilliant characters. He told me he had wanted to ask who I was as he recognised me. I think he was just being polite. I'll always remember his brilliant quote as Billy Bleach. 'She was half woman, half fish. Terrible in the kitchen, but a bloody good swimmer'. They don't write them like that anymore.

Anyway, back to my new best friend Alan. He was an incredible man, with an encyclopaedic knowledge of music and a wonderful positive outlook on life. He was also the inventor of the phrase CLANG!, the book title, as explained on page one. Alan had been in the business for donkey's years, and he could out clang anyone, and frequently did. On that evening at the beeb, halfway through the show, Alan pulled Mike aside to interview him and then did something I had never seen. He made Mike star struck. Alan turned to a television and asked Mike to watch it. Suddenly the four members of, CLANG! ... U2, were on the screen congratulating Mike on the thirty year anniversary of the debut album 'Declaration'. When they started singing the track 'Blaze of glory', he even started singing along. It was lovely seeing that side of him.

It happened again in 2019 when we went to see, CLANG! ... THE KILLERS, play an outdoor show at Cardiff Castle. Mike was talking to his mate as, CLANG! ... BRANDON FLOWERS, started singing The Alarm classic 'Rain In The Summertime'. I couldn't believe it, and looked at Mike. He hadn't noticed as he was chatting, but everyone around him had, and when he did put two and two together, he did the same thing again. He started singing along to his own song. A beautiful nervous reaction which was compounded when we went backstage to meet the band afterwards and they told him what an inspiration he had been to the band. You see, he's just like you and me that Mike Peters.

I was like a small child at that Killers show as my lovely friend Tina Clark, who is the Zildjian Cymbal artist liaison, knew their drummer, CLANG! ... RONNIE VANNUCCI, and was lovely enough to introduce me. What a beautiful man and awesome drummer he is.

I always get star struck meeting my favourite drummers. I remember being at a Zildjian Artist Day in London and, CLANG! ... NICK MASON, from Pink Floyd was there. I shakily shook his hand and was chuffed that he was a genuinely nice man. We had a lovely chat. The following year at the same out of work drummer get together, CLANG! ... GINGER BAKER, was there. I asked my pal Matt Priest from Dodgy to come with me to meet the mythical iconic figure. After a brief handshake Matt and I agreed Old Ginge wasn't a particularly nice man. We didn't have a chat. Mike was good pals with, CLANG! ... SLIM JIM PHANTOM, from the Stray Cats, and James Stevenson was in a band with, CLANG! ... CLEM BURKE, legendary Blondie drummer. It's never easy playing knowing they are at your show.

When we were in America, I got a double dose of starstruck drummer-itus. First time was when we supported Dire Straits in Nashville. I was watching the drummer and marvelling at his technique when I realised it was, CLANG! ... STEVE FERRONE. For you non-drummers, he has played with everyone from Tom Petty, to Duran Duran, to The Average White Band. I met him afterwards, shaking like a star struck teenager. He was actually really lovely and, just as I thought I had peaked, Mike told me he was doing a radio show the following evening with, CLANG! ... CHAD SMITH. Yes, our favourite Chili Pepper had a radio show and Mike was going to be his guest, and I was going too. Now, would Chad remember me from twenty years earlier in Australia? This could be tricky. We arrived the next evening and were shown up to the studios. Out came Chad and embraced Mike. Then he looked at me. He paused. I paused. Should I; shouldn't I? 'This is my drummer, Smiley' said Mike. Another pause. I plucked up some courage. 'We've met before.' Another pause. He looked me straight in the eye. 'In Australia, with Strummer.' Boom. I stopped holding my breath and gave my new best friend Chad a hug. It's not always easy being me.

Archive. Parc Des Princes stadium, Paris 2007. Supporting Muse and Biffy Clyro.

Archive. France 2019.

Saturday afternoon Archive tour sports centre!

The Alarm.
Glastonbury mud-fest
2016!

The Alarm 2018. Salt
Lake Flats. When it got
dark, it felt like being
on the moon.

The Alarm and the
legendary Ian McNabb. Wales 2018.

With Mike Peters MBE at the Alan Thompson memorial concert. Cardiff 2019.

Mike Peters MBE. Frontman, legend, and high jump champion!

Always good to stay close to your boss!

Bruce Foxton. Bass legend, and (another) high jump champion! Brighton Centre 2014.

Photograph courtesy of ©Derek D'Souza

From The Jam with the wonderful Keith Chegwin, 2015.

Mum and Dad ...

... Brothers, Darren and Martin, and Sister, Soobie. See if you can tell the twins apart! I still can't.

Georgia, Lola, Kezza, and Jack. Everything I could ask for in one picture.

My two worlds.

At work …

With The Alarm. Up on the roof. NYC 2019.

… and at play.

With Kezza … my soul mate. 2019.

## CHAPTER 27
## ... LOVE HOPE AND STRENGTH

Anyone who knows anything about the Alarm family will tell you a massive part of its make up is to do with health. Mike is a three times cancer survivor. He was only on number two when I joined the band. When the evil little blighter reared its ugly head again, we were out on a UK tour. The thing about Mike is he never really lets you know if he's feeling under the weather. He soldiers on until you realise he's hit a bit of a wall. I remember my first taste of this when we were recording at Abbey Road. He had decided to write and record the world's longest song. It was called 'The Scriptures' and based around the same four chords, and he had invited anyone who wanted to write words, be it lyrics or poetry, to be part of the recording. I had already done the drums at my studio the week before. The song was about an hour and a half long and I did it in one take. I must confess to getting pretty bored around the hour mark and throwing in little bits of famous drum patterns to relieve myself and see if anyone would notice. The usuals are in there. 'Walk this way', 'Sunday Bloody Sunday' etc. My best one was the theme to 'Only fools and horses' but because the track was slower nobody ever noticed, or no one actually listened to the whole ninety-minute recording. I know I never did.

Anyway, we only had Abbey Road for a day, with hundreds of guests from all over the place popping in to add their four minutes. As the day drew on, I remember asking Mike if he was OK. He clearly wasn't, but carried on until the very end, with the last breath he had left. It was very hard to watch. He was receiving chemotherapy once a month back then, and he would ring me on his way in, and then on his way home, as if he had popped into Morrisons to do a big shop. He never moaned once. When we played in Germany years later, he picked up a cold. Nothing to worry about unless you're a singer. He could hardly speak and after myself, James, and tour manager Randy Labrow, all suggested he cancel the show like most normal artists, he took to the stage solo, and told stories around his almost unrecognisable croaky versions of Alarm songs. The next day he couldn't say a word. Now when it was put on social media that the tour was cancelled, and the band were heading home due to Mike's ill health, all hell broke loose. There were candlelight vigils and prayers being said all over the globe. Poor old Mikey was at this point sat next to me on the bus watching the footy and commenting using sign language. I never told him about the candles.

The band was booked to play Glastonbury. I can remember it clearly as it was the night before the Brexit vote. Fifteen of us sat up and discussed the vote before bed. Fourteen were for remaining and one was for getting out. There was a general presumption of a land slide for remaining. I woke up at nine to my room mate Randy Labrow's wake up call. I'll never forget it. 'Morning mate, do you want a cuppa, we voted out and Cameron resigned'. Funny the things you remember eh? So, on to the muddiest Glastonbury on record. It was impossible to get from A to B. It was proving impossible to get the gear onto the site. It was definitely impossible to get from our stage to the Pyramid stage to see ZZ Top, but Mike and I made a very valiant effort. Wellies for everyone. Our gear actually turned up twenty minutes before we were due on stage. It was a mad panic, but so worthwhile for us, and for the ten thousand fans who made it a truly special occasion, if a bit muddy.

At this point Mike was being followed around by a BBC film crew, who were putting together a documentary about his life and health. Now the reason I remember this isn't because of the camera crew slogging their way backstage caked in mud. It was because of a chat I was having with Jules, Mike’s wife. Mrs P, as anyone who knows her or has come into contact with her will testify, is one of life's beautiful people, inside and out. Caring, giving and kind, with time for everyone and a constant smile on her beautiful face, as well as being funny as f**k, especially after a few beers.

We had met at a Los Mondo Bongo show at The Cavern in Liverpool and, after I serenaded her, before raiding the Alarm merch, we have been firm friends ever since. She is right at the top of the 'taking the piss out of Smiley' league, tucked in behind Kezza and Jain. She has always been at Mike's side, through sickness and in health. Like Mike, she had never moaned about the constant hospital visits and has remained Mike's rock. We were chatting at Glasto, in our wellies, when she told me of a hospital appointment she had the following day, to investigate a lump she had found after a routine check up. Surely the Peters’ couldn't be hit by lightening for a fourth time. Crushingly, it came to light that she had breast cancer.

Now I might get shot down for this, but I sometimes believe certain people in life are put in these situations because they are beacons of positivity for others who are maybe not so strong. My friend Jen was the same. Bubbly and vivacious, she told Kez and I about a headache she had had for days and couldn't get shot of. The next day, she was in surgery having a brain tumour removed. She was amazing. Positive to the last, a total inspiration to anyone who has had, or may have an illness. The positivity was a ray of light for everyone, and Jules was the same. She had to go to hospital everyday for a month and decided that the ten-mile round trip would be tackled on foot. The BBC film crew following Mike suddenly turned direction and the documentary became 'Mike and Jules'.

Now, the next turn in the Alarm road was quite radical. Craig was unavailable due to his commitments with The Mission. Mark had taken a lecturing post at a music school, and we had recording and live dates in place. Mike then made the decision to bring Jules into the band on keyboards, moving James onto bass with Mike himself covering all guitar duties. Meanwhile Jules was going through a long period of Chemo. In most people's world, getting asked to join a band at this point, as well as being a mother to two boys, would be out of the question. Not in Peters' world. She embraced the challenge and, suddenly, we were a four piece, recording new material and going out live. What people didn't immediately grasp was that Jules wasn't some Yoko Ono figure now walking by Mike's side, she is a grade eight pianist. The now re-styled band (always good having a girl in the band, men up their standards) was up and running, complete with three-part harmonies, and heading to America. Most fans loved the new line up. Some didn't, but then, you can't please everyone, so it's best to hedge your bets and go with the majority.

America, home of the free, the crazy and the downright scary. I've met so many characters, all with stories to tell and all, seemingly, with one thing in common. None of them voted for Trump. Anyone who did vote for him either live in the woods or don't come to Alarm shows. My two favourite things in the States are Truckstops and diners. You get all sorts of crazy shit in both. In the UK, your general BP petrol convenience will offer you the usual in calorific temptation; sweets, chocolate, crisps, ice cream etc. In the States you can buy all these things in a truck stop, as well as knives, bibles, coshes, medieval jousting helmets, and moose heads. I once got chatting to a nice lady with a lot of tattoos in the deep south. She was telling me she was married to a black man, and that three of his brothers had been killed by the Ku Klux Klan. 'That's why I carry this gun.' she said, as she pulled out something Clint Eastwood would have been proud of from her purse. 'Check please.'

Our travels across the States were in what's known as a 'bandwagon'. In reality, a huge RV style motorhome/truck which slept nine, and became home for two months of the year. I immediately took up my role as chief tea maker, with James on hoovering duties, and Jules on cleaning the toilet and telling us when the bin needed emptying. Trust me, without that woman's touch, and barking of orders, it would have looked like Neil's room in The Young Ones. There was something magical about the bandwagon. You felt safe in a world of nut bars. We gave up using dressing rooms and stayed on the bus, playing 'Saturday Night Fever' on full volume, as we danced around preparing for our show in true Alarm style. We used to park overnight in Walmart car parks. Most of them were open twenty-four hours, so it was brilliant fun walking around at three in the morning, buying stuff you would most probably regret in the morning. It became a bit of a game who could buy the most bonkers thing. I bought a Mutant Ninja Turtle Onesie, and I know James bought a battery powered hairdryer with free crimpers. That's how we rolled, usually after a second bottle of chardonnay.

The brilliant thing about America was that Mike and Jules knew so many people out there, we got to do really cool stuff. Their friend Blake, now my friend Blake, owns sixty-seven golf courses, so we played whenever we were near one, with a free breakfast for the non-golfers amongst us. We had a private tour of the White House courtesy of Elliot, who is a lawyer for the government. Boy could he tell a good Trump story. Then there were the musicians who popped up and joined us on stage. CLANG! ... TONY VISCONTI. The legendary David Bowie producer got up and played bass with us in New York. We met, CLANG! ... MELISSA ETHERIDGE, CLANG! ... BILLY IDOL, CLANG! ... TREVOR HORN, CLANG! ... CHRIS SHIFLET from The Foo Fighters, CLANG! ... DAVE PIRNER from Soul Asylum, and, CLANG! ... BOB GRUEN the legendary photographer, who took the famous New York City John Lennon photo. He had been big pals with Strummer, so it was such a pleasure to reunite with him and his wife twenty years after our last meet.

However, there were two highlights in our celeb meetings that were pure eighties royalty. Both in Los Angeles, the first was with, CLANG! ... TIFFANY. I was going to say 'I think we're alone now' but I was with James. The second, and still the best in my opinion was, CLANG! ... VANILLA ICE. We were playing a huge eighties show at the Microsoft theatre. Seven thousand people. We don't usually play those types of show, but this one seemed too good to turn down. I was standing outside the Vanilla dressing room, getting my photo taken next to his name on the door. A big burly security man came up and said,

'Hey man, you wanna meet the Ice?' Seriously, who wouldn't say yes? He said he would come find me when the time was right. Two hours later, he knocked on our dressing room door and said these mighty words. 'Are you ready to meet the Ice?' Yes, I was. He walked me to the dressing room and told me to stand and wait outside. Sure enough, after a few moments, out came the legend himself. He was huge. He was so handsome. He was so stoned. But he was also very gracious, and we had our picture taken. Why is he such a cool celebrity? Because he's Vanilla Ice.

Now add to the list of eighties legends, CLANG! ... GAZ TOP. In my youth, I had always been a fan of his, on my favourite kids TV shows, 'How' and, especially, 'Get Fresh', with Gilbert the Snot Monster. Gareth as he now refers to himself, or Gar, as I now do, came with us as compere on the last American tour, and was an absolute star. He is one of the few good souls in life who consistently put a smile on peoples faces, and tells a brilliant showbiz story, or after a few beers, many showbiz stories. I introduced him to the 3am Walmart stroll, and those mornings became more frequent and always entertaining. Bless ya Gar.

It was while we were in New York that I saw Mike Peters Superhero Powers at close quarters. We had all been on the Staten Island ferry and, as we disembarked, and the ferry pulled away, Jules realised her bag, complete with her favourite boots and a considerable amount of cash, but more the boots, were still on the now pulling away ferry. Quick as a flash Mike started running at full Superman pace along the river road chasing the ferry. When he was out of sight, we all did what you do in a situation like that. We went to the pub. Half an hour later, a heavily sweating MP appeared, with bag, complete with cash and more importantly, boots. He had out run the ferry to its next port. Now obviously I would have done the same in the circumstances, but he had beaten me to it. Show off.

He's always got a story to blow everyone out of the water. We went to see 'Bohemian Rhapsody' at the flicks in the States on a night off. As we were walking out of the cinema en route to a diner, Mike told a story about having met, CLANG! ... FREDDIE MERCURY, and even buying his piano. It put my Peter Andre story to shame.

The shows were always brilliant in America. I think we did over a hundred in one twelve-month period. I used to try and get memorabilia for Geordie Nigel. He loved a poster that lad. Halfway through an in-store performance at a record shop in New York State I noticed a, never before seen, rarity that he would love, pinned to the wall behind me. While Mike was singing a long intro to his classic 'Spirit of 76' and with the majority of the crowd singing along with their eyes closed in awe of the moment, I leaned back and slowly pulled the poster off the wall, rolled it up and popped it in my back pocket. What I didn't know was that the performance was being filmed and shown live back in the UK, so my little act of Geordie kindness was witnessed by all and sundry. After the show Nigel texted me. 'I hope that poster was for me bonny lad'.

The other fabulous thing about our American adventures was hooking up with my old Potato Joe brothers. We are all so scattered these days, but I got to see Andi in Nashville, Trevor in Vegas, and Mark in Miami. Having all been such big Alarm fans back in the day (and back about thirty chapters), bringing the boys in to meet Mike, Jules and James was a real pleasure for all of us. I am so grateful to those beautiful boys for everything they showed me in those early days. They, as much as anyone, are why I am where I am musically today.

Mike and Jules run a charity. A worldwide cancer charity called 'Love Hope Strength'. Its basic premise is to swab people at gigs to see if matches can be found for bone marrow transplants to treat blood cancer. They have had thousands of matches from all over the world and the charity grows ever bigger by the year. In 2018 they did a charity walk through the Grand Canyon. Myself and James, along with thirty others walked through the stunning canyon by day and sat round the camp fire, singing Britney Spears songs, by night. It was a cathartic experience and one I will never forget. The opportunity to see such a great wonder of the world close up, through wind, rain, sun, and snow, was such a pleasure to be involved in. Oh, and we raised a bit of lolly for 'charidy mate'. But we don't like to talk about it.

Life in Alarm world is bliss. As a musician, you feel appreciated and respected, and as a family we all love each other. It's Like The Partridge Family meets The Brady Bunch. Not sure which one James is in. A lot of that love comes from the friendships we have had in place for over a decade; but also because the bond with Alarm fans from all over the world is second to none. We are all, as they say, 'singing from the same hymn sheet'. Apparently, I've even got a special Alarm walk that was lovingly pointed out at last years Gathering. I'll add Geordie Nigel and my mate Tony Gibson to the piss taking league for pointing that one out. As for my Alarm family, they walk forever by my side.

# CHAPTER 28
# ... STUDIOS

Studio work is something I've loved doing since my teens. That first session at fourteen-years-old with Vox Humana, set me on a course that I've never looked back from. It's one of those things where you learn something new from every session. All artists are different, and record in unique ways. I've learnt so much in thirty-seven years, and I reckon I've recorded over a thousand songs. Some sessions were amazing, some enlightening, emotional and satisfying. Some were awful. There's a magic in a studio, just before you press the record button. You are about to create something brand new that will, hopefully, last forever, unless it's really shit and ends up in the bin. There's been a few but, luckily, not too many.

I was lucky at the start of my recording career to work with some amazing producers who helped me on the right track for future sessions. The legendary, CLANG! ... LARRY PAGE, who was famous for his work with hundreds of acts from the sixties and the seventies. Bands like The Kinks and The Troggs. He even produced the iconic 'Blue is the colour' that Chelsea fans still sing today. He had a classic sixties style. Sharp suits with huge glasses. A bit like Austin Powers. I loved working in the studio with Larry and learnt so much. I got into a situation with a band manager once, regarding song writing credits and Larry offered to help me. We went to a hotel in London and sat at a table. Larry ordered everyone drinks and was charming. Then down to business. His opening line of 'I read your contract and then I used it to wipe my arse' set the tone of the meeting. I walked out with fifty per cent.

I did a great session for, CLANG! ... TRACEY ULLMAN, with my pal Andy Marlow. She was writing the sketches for her BBC show, and Andy was putting the songs together with her. When it came to recording the drums, the songs were so funny I kept laughing during takes and had to redo them several times. It's not always serious. I did an album in Liverpool with, CLANG! ... IAN McNABB. He sat ten feet away from me with his guitar and microphone and with no rehearsal, played the songs at me and by the magic of eye contact and Scouse humour, we pretty much got everything first take. Genius. I wouldn't recommend going to the pub with him though. I think that hangover lasted three days. I'd rate his voice as good as anyones.

Not everyone works like that. Robbie used to moon at me while I was recording with him. We stayed at a studio out in the country once and sat in a field on the hay bails chatting till the sun came up. They sent a search party to find me, or was it the UK's biggest singing sensation? Who know's? Guy Chambers was a brilliant producer.

As was Martin Coogan, during my Mock Turtles days. One day his brother, CLANG! ... STEVE COOGAN, was round at the studio. It was during the time of his 'Tony Ferrino' character, and I ended up doing the drums on that well-known classic 'Fishing for girls'. I still say Martin is funnier than Steve.

Another fab producer is Ash Howes. He has gone on to produce everyone from Kylie to One Direction. I did some early recordings for a band called Hipjam at the studio owned by, CLANG! ... PHIL MANZANERA, from Roxy Music, with Ash. What I remember most about those sessions was that his house was next door, and it was round. I recently recorded some drums with him for, CLANG! ... ALEXANDRA BURKE, and, CLANG! ... NEWTON FAULKNER. It's strange that you play on these artists albums but never actually meet them. The same thing happened with french superstar, CLANG! ... MYLENE FARMER, and, CLANG! ... CARRIE GRANT.

My dream session came via a friend of Archive's bassist Jonathan Noyce. His name was Peter Lawler. The brief was amazing. We would be recording the new Premiership football theme, at Abbey Road. I had to pinch myself. Sure enough, the track, 'When Saturday Comes', was played before every match, and used as the theme tune around the world whenever Premiership football was shown. My Dad was especially proud of that one, and, whenever he went to Stamford Bridge, he told anyone within twenty rows to be quiet as his boy was drumming.

Another memorable session was once again through dear old David Enthoven. He was managing a wonderful girl singer songwriter called Hero Fisher. He asked me to go and sit in on a few rehearsals and cover a few shows. She was a special talent. They had half her album recorded and were planning the next sessions. They asked if I was free to record for a week, in Brooklyn. What a feeling, flying out to New York to record in a fantastic studio with such a fantastic artist.

A particularly wonderful session came in 2019, when The Alarm recorded at the legendary 'Sun Studios' in Memphis. The place was full of memorabilia from all the amazing artists who had famously recorded back in the Rock & Roll heyday. CLANG! ... ELVIS, CLANG! ... JOHNNY CASH, and

CLANG! ... JERRY LEE LEWIS; all were adorned on the wall. The piano Jerry used on Great Balls Of Fire was still there, Elvis' microphone, and as a 'Brucey bonus' for me, the drum kit, CLANG! ... LARRY MULLEN JR, used for, CLANG! ... U2, on the Rattle And Hum album. Now that my friends, is a session I will never forget.

Not all sessions were that great. I remember going to the house where, CLANG! ... 5 STAR, lived. Remember them? They were like a UK version of The Jacksons, until their Dad spent all their money. The house had to be sold, as did their cars. When we recorded there, the driveway was full of Lambourghini's and Ferraris. About a month later when I drove past, they had all gone, and there was a mini metro parked in the drive. Their studio was incredible, with walls that could revolve, and it had wood panelling on one side and carpet on the other, to totally transform the sound of the room. Sadly, when we were there, the money had clearly run out, as had the engineer, and nobody really knew how to operate the desk.

Another fabulous studio is The Barn in Ripley. Not just because it's owned by, CLANG! ... PAUL WELLER. It is just a brilliant place, full of Mod memorabilia. I played a session there once with, CLANG! ... STEVE CROPPER. I sat and asked him all about his career, and what it was like being in 'The Blues Brothers'. He was lovely; he had a show to do that night and, as he left, he was given two bottles of wine as a thank you. The story goes that he had drank both bottles by the time he got to his gig. Not his best performance by all accounts. My friend Charles is a brilliant producer and works for Weller. I pop in to see him occasionally for a cuppa and the last time, Weller answered the door. I froze for a second, starstruck, then luckily my brain told me not to say 'I live near you.' again, and we had a jolly nice chat. Alan Thompson thought that story was well worthy of a clang. Thommo loved Weller.

I decided to get myself a little recording set up, mainly, so that I could do drum sessions for people who were asking. I was living in a first floor flat at the time and the lovely landlady downstairs said it would be fine. Little did she know what a drum kit sounds like perched above your lounge when you're trying to watch Eastenders. We came to an agreement about when I could and couldn't make noise and I started recording drums for people. I gradually acquired more and more equipment and was struggling to live and record in the same flat. So, I moved in with Kezza and kept the flat as a studio. I was working more and more, and also branching into producing and writing.

Over the next year or so I honed my craft, working with more and more artists. Then out of the blue the lovely landlady told me she had reluctantly agreed for her son to move into the flat. I had six weeks to find a new place to record, and to put the mountain of studio equipment I had acquired. At the time Kez and I were having a new kitchen built by a jolly old builder called Simon. He loved, during his tea breaks, to chat with me about music, and when I told him of my predicament he put his tetley down and looked into the garden. It was quite a large garden with not a lot going on in it. He looked, scratched his chin, and did that measuring thing builders do with their fingers held up in front of their face. 'I'll build you a studio. Thirty-five square meters. Ten grand'.

There and then, SUNSHINE CORNER STUDIO'S was born, after I had rung my Mum to borrow the money.

Over the next six weeks I had all the neighbours knocking on the door asking what was being erected at the bottom of my garden. Very quickly the studio took shape, much to the annoyance of my lovely wife, whose kitchen was at that point, half finished. Six weeks later everything in the flat was moved to the new building. It took eight people to get the mixing desk out of the flat and another eight to get it into the studio. That's what friends are for. I wonder where they all are now. I named the studio after my late Grandfathers church club he used to run by the sea in Kent for kids in the school holidays. Sunshine Corner Studio's. A nice gesture for a wonderful man.

Word started to spread, and bands began to book in to record demos. Every session was a challenge. I now realised being a producer was like being a Psychiatrist. Some of those early sessions were a real learning curve, not just on microphone technique and the recording process, it was more the fact that the singer hated the drummer and the bass player would say no to every idea unless it was suggested by the guitarist. It was daunting, yet quite amusing, and a challenge I began to relish. I started to get the knack of gaining people's confidence, especially drummers. They all need an arm around them to tell them how great they are. They also need telling that half their drum fills are shit and they can't play in time. Always start with a positive. 'That fill you did in the middle was amazing, probably the best bit of drumming I've heard in the studio this year. That's the key part of the track for me. It really stands out and makes you sound amazing. I would lose ALL the other fills if I were you, just because that one is so good.' You'd be amazed how many drummers fell for that. Guitarists too. There's nothing more satisfying than getting a guitar player whose original solo consisted of more notes than there are stars in the sky to end up playing just one. 'You sound amazing man, one note, like Keith Richards!!' Yep, that worked too.

The bands were coming in thick and fast, and I was working on several albums at the same time. One band, who won't be named for legal reasons, were three quarters through their new album. They clearly didn't like each other and seemed destined to finish the record in order to split up. One night I decided to do a bit of editing. The next morning when I went back to finish, it was gone. The whole album. Wiped. Nothing saved in the computer. Nothing backed up. Gone. How was I going to get myself out of this one? I phoned Mike Peters. His answer, 'Fake a break in and say they stole your hard drive'. A good option some would say. Another alternative was a power failure that miraculously wiped everything. Another good option. I decided to try a different angle. I emailed the band to say I had been listening to the album and had come to the opinion that the songs were so good they needed recording again, to do them justice, and, as they were so good. I was willing to do this for free as I believed in the band so strongly. The band had a meeting to discuss my generous proposition. 'We are up for it, but would like to listen to what we have before we commit' Damn, plan B. 'I think we should start from scratch, you're a better band now than when you first started the album two years ago.' 'You've wiped the album haven't you Smiley?' 'Yes, I have.' There's a lesson for everyone right there, especially you Mr Peters. Honesty is a wonderful thing.

Sunshine Corner's first big name session came out of the blue. An old mate of mine from the Strummer days told me about a project called 'Jail guitar doors'. It was a venture which helped ex-prisoners, when released, get back on their feet via music and, particularly, recording. They wanted to record a 'charity single'. It sounded very worthwhile, so I offered the studio, and my services, for nothing. What I didn't know was, the three key players in the venture were, CLANG! ... BILLY BRAGG, and, CLANG! ... MICK JONES and CLANG! ... TOPPER HEADON from The Clash.

The first to arrive was Topper, one of my drumming heroes. We had a chat and he showed me a couple of old Clash tricks, such as how he played London Calling and Rock The Casbah. Fantastic drummer. Then some of the prison guys began arriving and we set everyone up ready to record. Suddenly, CLANG! ... JOHNNY GREEN, the famous Clash tour manager appeared with a couple of pals. 'Allo Smiley, make us a cup tea will ya sunshine' he said, sounding like Harry Grout out of Porridge. Then word spread to the studio that Billy Bragg was in my lounge having a lovely old chat with my wife, soon joined by Mick Jones. She didn't have a clue who they were but loved showing off our now, thankfully, finished kitchen. When the chaps had finally finished discussing our new hob, they joined us in the, now packed to the rafters, studio. My abiding memory was when Billy and Mick were singing together into the same microphone and I stopped the track to say it was slightly out of tune and would they mind doing it again. There was a sudden pause in the room. I thought Grouty was gonna 'put me six feet under'. Billy and Mick smiled, and we re-recorded. Suddenly I felt like a producer. I've got a lovely Thank You letter from Billy Bragg proudly displayed on the studio wall.

I didn't think that session could be topped until my friend Andy Lewis, himself a producer as well as being Weller's bass player, told me he was producing an album for, CLANG! ... MARK BUTCHER, the former England cricketer, and could he record it at Sunshine Corner, with me playing drums. Now being a massive cricket fan, this was too good to be true. Mark was lovely, but more surprising was just how good a singer, guitarist, and songwriter he was. 'Now Playing' is a brilliant album and firmly put the studio on the music, and cricketing map.

The one thing that everyone who ever recorded the studio had in common was BJ, our home and studio dog. He was a big old boxer who befriended every singer, guitarist, bass player, and anyone who could play an instrument. He also befriended their friends and anyone else who ventured in the studio. Everybody loved Beej. I would often turn around from the mixing desk to see him sprawled across three members of a band, or cuddled up to a singer. The one thing everyone also had in common was his flatulence. That dog could fart for England, and would regularly clear the studio. He was loved by everyone, is in so many band pictures and on many recordings. He is sorely missed. RIP Boy x

There has always been a strong Mod connection in the studio. There is memorabilia all over the place, including a huge Quadrophinia picture on the wall which is ironic for two reasons. The first was a track James Stevenson and I recorded as 'The

Cockney Alarm' with, CLANG! ... PHIL DANIELS. A punk version of 'Blue is the colour'. He is in the picture. The second was when The Transmitters were in recording and had invited down, CLANG! ... GARY SHAIL, to record a vocal on one of their tracks. Gary played Spider in Quadrophenia and was well impressed; he also had a place on the studio wall. I've used him since for voice overs. A great actor and charming man.

I must admit to being slightly nervous when the band 'Cow' came in to do their new album. The singer is Weller's cousin, and they had recorded their previous three albums at the Barn, with Paul's producer. How do you compete with that? The answer, you don't. They were a joy to work with and recorded a brilliant album 'Steeple For The People'. We've since recorded with the king mod himself, Mr Mike Dobie, who is already onto album number three, and, also, with the Magic Mod. Ben is a real friend of the stars and came in to record some tracks. He also kept my daughter and wife entertained with card tricks. Add to that sessions with the original Jam member Steve Brookes for his new album, and you get a pretty full set of mod royalty. There is of course one missing. Our friendship started with a phone call late one night.

'Is that Smiley? Hello mate, it's, CLANG! ... BRUCE FOXTON.'

## CHAPTER 29
## ... FROM THE JAM

It was like a game of musical chairs involving Big Country, The Alarm, and, From The Jam. The Alarm were out on a UK tour when Mike Peters announced that he had been asked to sing with Big Country. He liked the idea of getting his teeth into something new and, as he does with everything, immersed himself in the history of the band, learnt all the words and, of course, went shopping for check shirts. Meanwhile, Big Country hadn't really done anything for a while and their famously named drummer, CLANG! ... MARK BRZEZICKI (yes I googled the spelling) was playing drums with From The Jam, featuring original bass player, CLANG! ... BRUCE FOXTON, as well as Russell Hastings, in the Paul Weller chair.

I'd been a huge fan of Mark's during my teens, and studied his drumming style, which is still totally original to this day. I had met him a few times over the years, and my Mum has a picture of me with lovely long blonde hair playing his famous red Pearl drum kit, in her lounge. (The picture, not the kit, her lounge isn't big enough for Mark's kit, which is huge). Anyway, with Big Country announcing Mike as their new singer, The Alarm came off the road, and Mark told Bruce and Russell that he would be prioritising his band of thirty years over anything else, including them. By all accounts they were not particularly happy with this announcement, and promptly fired him whilst he was driving them to a show in Scotland. Amazingly, he still did the show.

Now, Mike being Mike, he saw an opportunity arising, and phoned me to ask if maybe I would be interested in the From The Jam vacancy. I'd loved The Jam at school. They were THE band for me, just like Imagination were to ninety-eight per cent of everyone else. The prospect of playing with Bruce Foxton was delicious, as he is generally regarded as a legend in the bass department. So, I told Mike I would love to. Sure enough, the following evening, while I was pottering around in my studio, the phone rang, and it was Bruce. We had a lovely chat about all things Jam, bass, and drums, and he finished with the immortal lines 'Well you can talk the talk, let's see if you can walk the walk.'

A few days later, we all met in a very small rehearsal room. I had been given my list of Jam songs to learn, and had really got my head stuck into them. They really are some of the best songs ever written. So, there I was, sat behind my kit with Foxton on my left and Hastings on my right. First song on the list, 'Going Underground'. What a way to start your audition process. It was amazing hearing the bass played in that way, and I was slightly star struck but instantly locked in with the boys. This was going to work. After three hours of rehearsals, I was driving home and got a call from Bruce offering me the job for X amount of money. Very nice, very professional I thought. Ten minutes later, Russell called to offer more money than Bruce. I liked this job already. The first show was two weeks away in Woking, so I started learning.

The set was made up of half well-known hits; Town Called Malice, Eton Rifles, etc, and half album tracks. Luckily, I knew them all, so delved into the drum parts and really learnt them. The day of the first show came and I turned up separately as it was pretty local to where I lived (as Paul Weller will testify). I met the crew, and then we ran through a soundcheck. Everything seemed to be in order. I even knew the support band, 'The Ska Souls', who would later come and record two albums at my studio, so the omens were good. I was slightly nervous as I didn't want to make any mistakes on my debut. I then realised my nerves were nothing compared to Bruce and Russ. As I would later find out, their whole gig day was based around routine and repetitiveness, which basically meant they started getting nervous from about three and didn't chill out until they were back in the hotel bar.

Anyway, back to the show. It went really well. I was so pleased I had nailed everything I had put the hours into learning, and walked back into the dressing room, expecting high fives and congratulations. What I got was the now legendary response 'Yeah, just a couple of things Smiley.' Now this response was a huge favourite in the Archive camp. They found it hilarious, and would call me after shows for an update on the latest 'couple of things'. Don't get me wrong, I'm all for constructive criticism, but when you've just learnt twenty four songs and had one rehearsal, the fact that there's a push in the third verse of 'Little Boy Soldiers', and a pause in the second chorus of 'When You're Young', are quite small parts of the musical jigsaw. I personally would have played on the ninety-nine per cent success rate as opposed to the one per cent negative. Hey ho, each to their own. Between the next couple of FTJ shows I was in rehearsals with Archive, and they found it extremely funny to say after a few run throughs, 'Yeah, just a couple of things Smiley.' The gag that keeps on giving.

So, I was juggling Archive and FTJ nicely enough, but had informed Bruce and Russ of my upcoming Archive festivals dates for which I would be unavailable. They looked perplexed, slightly unsure of what I was saying. Turns out they are not big on drummers not being available all of the time, so when I was playing golf with my Dad the following day, I got a call from Bruce, as I was just about to birdie the third. 'Yeah hi mate, we've decided to go with Tom on drums. All the best'. Now, Tom was actually the occasional keyboard player in From The Jam, but could hit things with sticks as well, and was available, a lot. So that was that. I had enjoyed my brief time with the chaps and promptly went on to miss my putt, with my Dad blaming Bruce for putting me off. Bless him. So loyal.

Archive finished their summer of festivals and were thought to be heading out in the autumn for a tour. En route into rehearsals in London one morning I was just stepping into the studio when the phone rang. 'Smiley it's Bruce. Tom can't do our autumn tour and we were wondering if you were available?' I popped my head into the studio and saw Darius. 'Are we still doing shows in the autumn?' 'No mate, next year now.' 'Yes Bruce, I'd be delighted to.' My autumn diary was once again full. Just.

The tour was celebrating the classic Jam album 'All Mod Cons'. It's a brilliant record, but I needed to learn it parrot style to give it its uniqueness. I did a lot of prep for the tour and we headed out on day one after a weeks-worth of rehearsals. What struck me early was the similarity in the fans to the Strummer days. The Clash and The Jam are similar animals, some saying The Jam carried on from where The Clash left off. The fans, once again, knew more than I.

I began to get used to the 'From The Jam' way. They ran a tight ship. There were the three of us, who travelled together in a hire car. Then there was a sound man and a tech, who travelled on ahead of us and were ready for our arrival, usually standing to attention at the door. We would arrive at our hotel, usually an hour or two before our soundcheck, and meet up in the lobby fifteen minutes before our due time. Then, dressing room, stage, soundcheck, and back to the hotel. We would then meet in the bar approximately forty-five minutes before we were due to leave for the show. That would mean three bottles of beer for me and Bruce, and lime and soda for Russ, as he didn't drink. We would then drive to the gig, be met at the stage door by the tech, and drink one more beer. Bruce and Russ would nervously run through songs they knew like the back of their hand and had played hundreds of times. Then, quick group hug, and bang, showtime. This all sounds quite meticulous but that's the point, it was. Everyday, the routine was the same. That's how they rolled.

After the first couples of shows we were past the 'just a couple of things Smiley' and into a groove. The next realisation was the hotel scenario. This was one of the highlights of being in the band. You see, the chaps would take it in turn to book the hotels, so would try to outdo each other, but strictly within budget, a generous budget I grant you. No Premier Inns in FTJ world. Poor Lenny Henry. Bruce was very particular about his room. Many was the time I would come downstairs for the three-forty-five soundcheck lobby call, only to find he had changed rooms three times. It could be anything from the colour of the wall, a south by south westerly direction, or lack of custard creams. It really started to amuse me, and every day was a new adventure in hotel world. My favourite two hotel memories are pure comedy genius. The first was at a big old four star in Devon. I got my key and walked up to my room, bidding the boys farewell for two hours. It was a Saturday so the first thing I did was put 'Talksport' on and listen to the football. My view was sensational. It looked out across the ocean, sparkling in the autumn sunlight like a David Hockney painting. Sublime, and with Chelsea two up on West Ham, the day just couldn't get any better. I headed down for our pre-soundcheck rendezvous and found the chaps in deep discussion in the ballroom, which also looked out to sea. Beautiful. They were having a right old moan so, to lighten the mood I said 'Blimey, even you two can't complain about the ocean view from the bedroom.' It was at this exact point that I realised, as Bruce's head slowly turned towards me like that girl in the Exorcist, that neither he, nor Russ, had the same view as me. They had the car park. The silence was defining. Nothing was said and I didn't think anything else of the incident until the following day when we were checking into our next hotel in the Wiltshire countryside. The concierge greeted Russell with a welcoming smile and when told of who we were said 'Ah yes, three supreme doubles'. Russell's reply was hilarious. 'No, that's now changed to two supreme doubles, and a single'. Yes folks, I had had a hotel demotion.

The best was yet to come when we booked into, what can only be described as, a B&B. Cosy, warm, with custard creams and bourbons. What's not to like I thought? I made my way to my small room (still in the demotion stage at this point) and settled in for two hours before our usual lobby meet. After a relaxing book reading sesh, I made my way to the lobby. There was nobody there. I looked into the car park and there was no car. Very strange. I checked my watch. This was unusual to say the least. I began to wonder what was going on. Suddenly, the car pulled into the car park with Bruce and Russell in the front. I got in the back and nothing was said. Maybe they'd nipped to Sainsbury's. Anyway, soundcheck routine was as per usual, and an hour later we pulled away, heading back toward the B&B. As we got about a mile away, Russ took a sudden left turn. Through a leafy driveway appeared a great big green and white sign with two words. Holiday and Inn. 'Me and Bruce didn't like the other place, so we've booked in here. You take the car and pick us up at seven-forty-five. OK?' Before I could take stock of the situation, Bruce hit me with the best line yet. 'Here you are mate,' handing me a key with a 9 attached to it, 'have my room, it's bigger.' Yes folks, I had not only had my room made smaller, I was now in a different hotel, or should I say, B&B.

## CHAPTER 30
## ... THE START OF THE END

Despite my hotel demotion, things seemed to be going well in From The Jam. There was steady work in the diary. I simply got in the back of the car, usually on a Thursday morning, and was dropped off at an adjacent, but not necessarily handy for me, train station on Sunday afternoon. Normal service had been resumed in the hotel stakes, unless Tom was on the gig playing keys, then we would share. I liked Tom a lot, but I think sharing a hotel room in your mid-forties is a bit weird. Occasionally, I was asked to drive. The first time was hilarious. It was a long motorway run and almost immediately after taking the wheel, the boys were asleep. The radio was on to keep me company, but at a volume you would need one of those old hearing trumpets to hear. I was trying to guess the answers in Pop Master, but every time I sneaked the volume up a notch, Russell, without opening his eyes, would knock it down again, two notches, just to make a point. Annoying really, as I was already on twenty-one points and heading for the three in one. After a few hours I pulled into a service station as requested by Bruce and his bladder. Then the boys hit me with another classic FTJ quote. 'We've been watching your speed.' (with their eyes shut). 'We usually like to keep it somewhere between the seventy-nine and eighty-one mark.' 'So, about eighty then?' 'Yep that should do it.' Genius.

There seemed to be a bit of an Eastenders connection with the band. Bruce was good mates with, CLANG! ... SHANE RICHIE, who we saw on regular occasions. When we played in London, we were serenaded from the royal box, not an actual royal box, but the posh seats nearest the stage, like the ones Waldorf and Statler from The Muppets used to sit in. Anyway, that night was full of Eastenders royalty. I'll go with character names as I don't know their real names or, to be honest, really care. So, we had, CLANG! ... BILLY MITCHELL, CLANG! ... KAT SLATER, and, CLANG! ... IAN BEALE. They were all very nice and obviously big Jam fans. Billy Mitchell asked me to go to his house and give him some drum lessons. I didn't.

At one show I broke a stick mid song. Now, as a drummer, when a stick breaks you literally have a split second to react. Your choices are usually dictated by the severity of the break. This particular evening the stick fractured in the middle of a fast Jam track and, having a split second to get rid and pull out a new one from my stick bag, I launched the broken one toward the audience but holding back as to not twat some innocent Jam fan on the noggin. Famously, in the eighties, Madonna's drummer threw a stick into the crowd and it took a fan's eye out, and he was sued for a million.

So, my aim was the gap between the stage and the crowd. As I launched, I noticed Russell had a half-drunk diet coke can perched perilously near his left footed moccasin. It was too late. The stick flew directly into the can, the sugar free brown loveliness flew out of the can and onto the shoe. If looks could kill. After the show I tried to explain to Russ that if I tried to hit the can another hundred times, I probably wouldn't hit it once. He was having none of it. Goodbye supreme double. Hello single. Another great onstage memory was when someone threw a drink on the stage. It didn't happen often but, when it did, all hell broke loose. On this particular occasion the drink hit Bruce square in the chest. He stopped dead in his tracks and, with a hint of Strummer, demanded to know who it was. A helpless punter was sacrificed by his former friends and security moved in to evacuate him. While this was going on, I was calling Bruce to get his attention. He finally turned around and said, 'What Smiley!?' I pointed out they were throwing out the wrong guy. I had seen who had thrown the drink, and he was currently shirking behind a tall chap, while the innocent one was being dragged out by his ears. I then had to stand up and point to the guilty water splasher, much to the amusement of the crowd. The man with the sore ear was reinstated by security and the guilty one led away, mouthing the word 'grass' at me. Bruce turned and looked at me and shrugged his shoulders, with the words, 'well that was fun'. Russ joined in the chuckles. Priceless.

Through the summer we got to play some 80's festivals. These were awesome, not just for the huge crowds and fantastic shows, but for one of my favourite hobbies, observing the ageing process. We were surrounded by artists I watched in their pomp, thirty-odd years ago, and let's just say it was fascinating trying to work out out who'd had a bit of work done on their face, who'd had a hair weave, and most enjoyably, who looked ropey as f**k. Now the exception to this rule was, CLANG! ... RICK ASTLEY. Not only did he look exactly the same as he did in the eighties, he had his own barnet, and was a truly lovely bloke. The only other celeb who ticked all those boxes was the positively wonderful, CLANG! ... KEITH CHEGWIN. What a lovely chap. We sat for ages chatting, and he really was just the same as the TV persona we all loved. I was genuinely sad when he passed away. Beautiful man.

There seemed to be a bit of a theme occurring, regarding support bands at FTJ shows. The prize for them all at the end of the day was, let's face it, a picture with Bruce. Time that picture right, and they would be walking home with a, soon to be framed, memory of a night they would never forget. Time it wrong, and their dreams could be somewhat shattered. You see, Bruce and Russ never rushed after a show. They were in their world and anyone, be it a support band, fan, or even a close family friend, was strongly advised to adhere to this. If you knocked on the dressing room door and proceeded to open it, the chances were that Bruce, standing in his pants, would not be in the most welcoming of moods, and you may well have blown your chance of your photo/autograph combo. Wait forty-five minutes and, the fully dressed and refreshed, From The Jam were nothing but courteous and forthcoming. I took it upon myself to seek out the support bands earlier in the day and advise them of the situation. Most took my advice, and the evening turned out splendidly. Some didn't. They don't have a photo or an autograph, just a distant memory of Foxton's Calvin Klein and sock combo, and a seven-letter send off!

One of my favourite support bands who played with us were 'The Transmitters'. A lovelier bunch of chaps you would struggle to find, and a mighty fine band to boot. They played with us a few times and I realised how good they were. Later, they would come to my studio on several occasions, to record EP's and an album. One sweaty gig in Manchester, we finished our set on a red hot hot evening, and as we gathered ourselves at the side of the stage, ready for the encore I was, literally, dripping with sweat. My shirt was wringing, and I spotted David Lees, singer with The Transmitters. Quick as a flash he spotted my predicament and offered me one of his band's t-shirts. A lovely gesture which, when we walked back out on stage was given a huge cheer by their local following. The encore was superb and, after an hour of dressing room decorum was respected, pleasantries were exchanged, and myself, Russ and Bruce made our way back to the hotel and ordered some well earned drinks. A few shiraz's and enjoyable conversation later and it was time for bed. Hugs were shared and I retreated to my room. I noted it was 2am and set my alarm for nine, to take full advantage of the free breakfast. When I was awoken seven hours later, I composed myself and went through the usual routine pre-breakfast. The last of these, post shower and dental care, was checking messages on my phone. I spotted an email, sent at 2.05am from Mr B. Foxton. It read as follows 'Fantastic show tonight bud, really enjoyed it. Don't ever wear a f*****g support band t-shirt on my stage again. Sleep tight'. The art of modern-day communication.

Later that year we went out on tour performing the legendary Jam album 'Setting Son's'. Tom was on keys, so I was back to sharing a room and sleeping in a single bed, like I did when I was fourteen. It went swimmingly well, apart from a few cancelations due to colds picked up by our leaders. While we were soundchecking, Bruce and Russ were working on new material for their upcoming album of original songs. I played along and the songs were sounding very promising. They told me they were planning to book into Weller's studio in the New Year to record. Happy days. I went home for Christmas looking forward to the upcoming sessions at The Barn. New Year came and went, and we did a few shows with the mighty, CLANG! ... NINE BELOW ZERO, supporting. What a great band. So professional. They never walked in on

Bruce in his pants. Mentions of upcoming studio dates had gone quiet so I sat back and waited for the call. When the phone rang, it wasn't the story I was expecting. Guy Helliker, who I had grown very close to in his role as website guru called. He had interesting news. Bruce and Russ were indeed in the studio. There were drums involved. Clearly not mine. Those of Mark Brzezicki. I was confused. Was I out? Was Mark in? I asked Mike Peters. He was none the wiser.

The following Saturday we headed to a gig in Newcastle, and decided to travel by train. I sat opposite Bruce and Russ for six hours. The studio wasn't mentioned. Now what would you do in that situation? Ask them directly, just before you pop to the drinks cart to grab three latte's, or keep your mouth shut. I was torn. It was a bit of an elephant in the room so I decided to break the ice. 'I see you saw Mark.' The pause was gloriously deafening. I had to stifle my inner giggling as the two of them sat opposite me trying to dig themselves out of their hole. Eventually, I got the pre-determined response (pre-determined while I got the coffees in) 'Yeah, we were finishing off old tracks from the last album, be good to get you in on a few tracks.' I decided not to hold my breath, for fear of dying.

Archive were regrouping and planning tours to accompany their new album, which I HAD played on (yes, Bruce and Russell, it really is that easy). I informed the FTJ hierarchy of the Archive plans. I knew the clock had started ticking. When I next saw the chaps, we discussed the situation, and I suggested Tom as the perfect drum dep scenario. Tom had ducked out of a few keyboard appearances and was not in the good books. So, I put forward a list of potential drummers who could easily fill my Smiley shoes when I wasn't available. Apparently, there was an audition of some sort with a few of my drummer friends reporting back on a rather negative vibe. Russell then informed me he had found a local chap to him, Mike Someone, who had performed well enough to be offered the Australian dates I couldn't do. Mike Someone came to our next show and I offered him everything he would need, be it advice or the use of my drums and cymbals if he was covering any UK shows. In my mind we were sorted. He could dep all the shows I wasn't available for across the summer, as Archive were doing huge festivals across Europe. Everyone was happy. While I was away in Germany, FTJ were nearing the end of their trip down under. I received a message from Mike Someone, informing me that he was now unavailable for any of the FTJ shows across the summer. My master plan was suddenly not looking so clear.

Over the next couple of spring months, we carried on with gigs as per usual, with no mention of the summer of conflict. One Monday morning I had an urge to call Russell. 'Hi Russ, hope you're well. What are your plans for the shows I'm unable to do this summer?' His answer, 'What shows?' 'The Archive festivals which clash with your shows, there are four.' 'Don't know anything about them Smiley.' I realised that, as they say in the musical world of dates clashing, the shit was about to hit the fan. I reckoned I just about had enough time to make a cup of tea before Russ had called Bruce and Bruce called me. Kettle boiled, water in cup, tea bag stirred, in the bin, milk added, ring ring. 'Smiley, it's Bruce, what the f**k's going on?' It was the start of the end. How we had got here is for you to work out. The words 'head in the sand' come to mind. It was just a matter of time before my phone rang again. Sure enough, later that afternoon, the bands agent called. I swear this was how the conversation went, word for word. 'Hi mate, it's Peter. Been speaking to the boys about the shows. We've spoken to Mike Somebody about depping for you, but he says he will only do the shows if he is offered the job permanently. So, we have. Good luck with everything.' That, my friends, was how my adventure in From The Jam world ended. I enjoyed it immensely.

I have great respect for Bruce and Russ. They have cornered their market, and are brilliant at what they do. Myself and Tony went to see them recently in Reading, and they were really good, and very friendly when we met up afterwards, forty-five minutes after the show, obviously.

Would I play with them again? Yeah. Would they ask me? Depends if they've read this book.

## CHAPTER 31
## ... SONG WRITING

I didn't really start writing songs properly until I had joined The Mock Turtles. I'd dabbled with a few ideas, usually with Aussie Mick next to me, reliably encouraging, whilst eating Monster Munch, and asking what time we were going to the pub. My dabbling came to fruition when, CLANG! ... MARTIN COOGAN, told me he would like to hear what I had in my locker. I borrowed an old four track machine and began layering drum machine, guitar, bass and piano. I sent him a couple of instrumentals which I thought he might quite like, but when he came back raving about one, saying he had written words and melody and that we now had a Mock Turtles song called 'Johnny Seven', I suddenly realised I might be on the right track. Aussie Mick was chuffed and suggested we went away for a few days, just us and the four-track, near a pub. So, we did; and came away three days later with seven completed tracks that were duly sent to Manchester.

Confidence really is the key with song writing. I have people coming in the studio week after week missing one key ingredient in their songs. Belief. If you are positive and complimentary, singer songwriters will generally then pull another albums worth of, as yet, untitled gems for your now positive perusal. I knew I could write to a point, but after my Coogan experience I realised what I needed was a co-writer, someone to ying my yang, Lennon my McCartney and Benny my Bjorn. At the beginning of the new millennium that man was Jonny Wilkes. Not Robbie's, famous for being Robbie's mate, Johnny, who I introduced you to earlier in the book as the singer with Slamm. My Johnny (you know what I mean) was no longer shlepping his way around the country, miming his way to a near Top Of The Pops appearance, he was working for a record company.

The discussion about co-writing came up over a pint in the, now sadly bulldozed, but still best named pub, The Dog and Fireside, in Virginia Water. I used to play there on acoustic nights, and Johnny often got up to share a few Crowded House classics with me. The landlady was very hospitable, and offered us the back room to sit and write in, and also provided lunch; on the house. We instantly connected and the songs started flying out of us. Very soon we had an albums-worth, and Johnny suggested a producer friend of his who had offered us studio time with a view to a third of the writing credits. Sounded like a good deal to me and we soon had an album, Smiley's People, in the bag, with most of the instruments played by ourselves, with a few guests thrown in. We gently passed it around and a few people showed a bit of interest. The same question kept appearing. 'When are you playing live?' We had no intention at that point of doing anything live and decided to crack on writing and recording. Six months later we had a second album in the bag, with a management team on board, all still saying the same. A band was needed.

A band was assembled. The band was named, after many meetings, 'One Iota'. We played some shows, started getting record company interest. Management made decisions. Promises were made. The band morphed over a period of a couple of years into a different line-up, and became newly named, as 'King Louie'. Finally, everything the management had asked for was there. New EP, photos, stylist, gigs. We were ready. Then we split up.

A few years later I decided to write a solo album. Not to reinvent the wheel, but just because I could. I wrote ten songs, borrowed an eight-track recorder and recorded everything myself. Two months later it was it my hand. I say it, a hundred CD copies of it. The album was titled, 'Don't Choke On Your Halo My Dear'. Looking back, the title was probably the best thing about the album, but there were definitely some positives, which would later lead to more albums, and initially opened the studio door.

When Sunshine Corner Studios was opened, and I started producing bands and singer songwriters, I quietly hid away when they had left, usually till the early hours, experimenting with sounds and song writing techniques. At this evolving time in my creative life, Kezza was an absolute star and, basically, left me to it.

So, a few years into the studio life I decided to record a new album. I did a few co-writes with various musician friends, Marc Hockley, Matt Round, and John James Newman. I demoed the tracks, playing everything myself, then decided to try using different, and better musicians than I. This was to open my eyes massively to future recordings. As much as I can play bass or guitar, a bass player or guitarist will invariably bring something extra to the track and, let's face it, play it better. I started scratching the surface to see who would be interested in being involved. What shocked me was the positive yes's I received from everyone.

On the first of the Smiley's Friends album I managed to use, CLANG! ... MIKE PETERS, CLANG! ... CHESNEY HAWKES, CLANG! ... PABLO COOK, as well as, CLANG! ... JONATHAN NOYCE from Archive, and CLANG! ... GARY NUTTALL, still in Robbie's band. I also discovered the greatest backing vocalists on the planet. Kerry Schultz and Dorie Jackson are a musical phenominum. Both are amazing singers in their own right; both are truly hilarious and gorgeous to be around in the studio, but most importantly, put them together and they sound like a choir. It's astonishing. The lead vocal situation would change throughout the six Friends albums. I sang six of the first album's tracks, called 'Smiley's Friends In High Places'. The rest were shared between Marc Hockley, Gary Nuttall, Chesney, Kezza, and John James Newman. What surprised me even more was the positive reviews and reaction the album received.

It was so easy to do, owning my own studio, that work on album number two started pretty much immediately. 'Smiley's Friends In Far Out Places' changed direction due to two reasons. I was now conscious that people wanted to be part of it, so I was getting more confident in who I asked. As well as the, now cast in stone, studio friends Kezza, Dorie, John James Newman, and Dale Davis, were guests including CLANG! ... MARTIN COOGAN, CLANG! ... RICHARD ARCHER, and, incredibly, CLANG! ... BRUCE FOXTON.

I was out on the road with From The Jam at the time, and asked Bruce if he would be interested in playing bass on a track called 13. 'Send me the demo and I'll have a listen' was his reply. 'Whats the worst that could happen?' I thought. Three days after I had sent it I'd heard nothing, and was conscious about it being the elephant in the room. We met up for another run of FTJ shows and nothing was said. Then in the bar before a show, Bruce said he had listened to the song. He said it was great, with a huge surprised look on his face, as though that fact had confused him. Anyway, he was planning on working on it in the coming week. Seven days later he sent me a home recording of him playing along and it was stunning. What really surprised me was how humble he was when I told him how great it was. Being such a perfectionist, he was desperate for it to be perfect. He agreed to come into Sunshine Corner and record it properly. The next day at noon, Bruce Foxton was sat next to me, recording bass on my song. Incredible. There was a beautiful moment. The chords in the chorus were B minor and A, and Bruce kept playing F sharp. At first it sounded a bit strange but then it really brought something different to the track. I asked him why, when the chorus was in B minor, he was playing F sharp? His answer? 'Cos I'm Bruce Foxton.' Genius. As the outro chorus approached, I suggested he follow the original chord sequence to break the cycle. 'Why should I do that?' Bruce inquired. 'Because I'm Smiley, and it's my song.' was my cheeky response. We tried it and it worked brilliantly. He was dead pleased with his part in the album and once again surprised me when he told me how good the whole album was. His wife loved it too. Job done.

The other change for the album was using a lyricist. A chap called Graham Turner was recommended to me by a friend and we soon got into a groove of me sending him songs, with some already written lyric ideas and music, and him finishing the track. The partnership worked well for three albums.

Album number three, 'Smiley's Friends On Sunshine Corner' was hot on the heels of its predecessor. This one featured all the usual suspects, as well as, CLANG! ... KAI STEVENS (Hard Fi), and, CLANG! ... ROBIN FOSTER, as well as a cameo appearance from my daughter Lola, as well as my dog BJ. A huge presence at this point was that of Alan Thompson. As mentioned in earlier chapters Al was a DJ at BBC Radio Wales. Suddenly I had found my muse. Someone who would listen to everything, and invariably come back with glowing positives. What an effect he had on me as a writer, but also as a person. I started pushing the boundaries with the songs and the guests, and Alan was right there with me. The usual scenario would be me recording till the early hours and sending him a copy of the latest piece. In the morning, as I started the pre-school run routine of dragging Lola out of bed and making Kez a cuppa, I would read Alan's critique, usually pages long, but so beautifully positive in every way. What an amazing man he was, and we became firm friends. I took the album out live for a show in London, which went extremely well. It opened my eyes to the live prospects.

The song 'End Of The World' was picked for a TV show, and I received a call asking if Graham and I would like to be interviewed. The basic premise was that it was about songwriting, and different well-known writers and producers would critique various songs until there was a winner. The Brucie bonus was that it was being presented by the former Radio one DJ, CLANG! ... MIKE READ. One evening he came to the studio, with a camera crew, and he couldn't have been nicer. We then filmed a piece where we visited, CLANG! ... WARREN BENNETT. He was a renowned producer as well as being the son of the legendary Shadows drummer Brian Bennett. We instantly hit it off and had a really enjoyable day at his stuido, once again being interviewed by Mike Read. The song was critiqued by people like, CLANG! ... CATHY DENNIS, and, CLANG! ... DAVID GRANT. We appeared in several episodes and, apparently, came second. To me music isn't a competition, so I lost interest very early. Graham still dines out on it.

The premise for album number four, 'Smiley's Friends Eclectic' was to use a different singer on every track. So, Alan and I gathered together a wish list, and we went fishing for singers. Some said yes, some didn't. We ended up with a gorgeous assortment of singers, the, still set in stone, friends, Kezza, Dorie, and John, again using Chesney too, but enlisting new faces including, CLANG! ... IAN McNABB, CLANG! ... OWEN PAUL, CLANG! ... ROBERT HART, CLANG! ... SAM BLUE, as well as, CLANG! ... DAVE PEN & HOLLY MARTIN (from Archive), and, CLANG! ... ELIZABETH WESTWOOD (from Westworld). Also, on the album was a cover of David Bowie's 'Moonage Daydream', which featured, CLANG! ... JAMES STEVENSON.

With a slight change in the songwriting department for the fifth album, lyricist duties were now shared between myself and John James Newman. Songs were being written in the summer sunshine in the garden after our respective school runs, demoed between us, and then sent to our muse, with Big Al coming back with all the positivity of a Chelsea fan hearing Big Frank was coming back as manager. The next album was really taking shape. We had some great guests on board, including Quadrophenia actor, CLANG! ... GARY SHAIL, as well as Happy Mondays percussionist Lea Mullen, guitar legend Jolyon Dixon, bassist's Russell Carr and Matt Round, as well as Tony Visconti's very talented daughter Jessica Lee Morgan. The Friends were now a live act, and we did several memorable evenings with varying line ups. The happiest band ever to walk the earth.

I had written a new song called 'Real Love'. It was very Beatlesque and I sent the demo to Alan. He begged me to let him play bass on it, so a day later, the Welsh McCartney had sent me the most sublime bass line. I then started writing a new song called Prophecy. It was really coming together, and I managed to get, CLANG! ... CRAIG ADAMS from The Mission, on bass. Alan was buzzing, saying it was my best track yet. I had the whole song written and recorded apart from one missing line, which I just couldn't get. 'Why don't you ask The King?' That was Big Al's nickname for Mike Peters. The next day The Alarm were playing in Liverpool and we were all in the dressing room. I told Mike about my predicament. 'Read me what you have, and I'll see if I can help.'

'Standing together, we can be strong enough, Standing forever.'

Mike then said calmly from the other side of the dressing room, 'We are nothing, without love.' That last line finished the song. Genius.

A few days later I finished the recording and sent it to Alan before I went to bed. When I went downstairs the following morning, for tea and school run duties, I checked my phone. He had sent a wonderful message, not only saying how the song was, in his words, a masterpiece, but how it epitomised optimism. He told me a story about a work colleague of his who had just been found dead at his home, the reason unclear. He pointed out how vital it was that we hold onto what we have in our lives, as we never know when it will all end. Beautiful words. So positive about everything. I had finally found a man who shared my vision, who listened with the same ears and looked at life through the same eyes. We could have been brothers.

Alan died three days later.

On a wet Thursday evening, a few days afterwards, John James Newman and I sat, quietly, in the studio. It was a strange feeling; we didn't really speak. We sat opposite each other with two guitars and two bottles of wine, and just started playing. We wrote a song called 'Afterglow', dedicated it to Alan, and the next evening, after I had recorded the music, John, Kezza, Dorie, and I, all stood around the microphone and sang in unison. The words said it all.

'Live your life, don't let go, keep love close. Hold on tight, shine your light, in the afterglow.'

What saddens me most is that he never got to hear the song.

A few months later I got a call from BBC Wales asking if I would like to perform at a memorial concert in Cardiff for Alan. The bill was great, with heavyweights like, CLANG! ... ANDY FAIRWEATHER LOW, and, CLANG! ... MARTIN STEVENSON. I was honoured to be asked, but felt I needed a little surprise up my sleeve for the evening. I went on and sang four of my songs that Alan had championed before reading out a message from, CLANG! ... IAN McNABB. I then told the audience how Al and I had met, and that it would only be fitting to finsh my set with a legend. CLANG! ... MIKE PETERS, joined me onstage, nobody knowing he was there, and we duetted on three songs for our friend. A night I will never forget.

The 'Afterglow' album was very popular within the Friends world, many saying it was their favourite, but for me it was tinged with sadness and loss. What brought it alive was when we played it live, a wonderful evening in Ascot which was attended by friends from way back to the present day. 'Prophecy' was especially relevant that evening.

Album number six was hard to record, without my muse and his confidence building morning messages over tea-making and Lola-waking. I wrote a lot of it while in America with The Alarm, and with John when I got back. I tried to get away from the feelings of loss that engulfed Afterglow, and John and I moved towards a more upbeat feel-good direction. 'Smiley's Friends In The Sixth Sense' proved popular in America via The Alarm tours and across the board got the best reviews yet. It was a pleasure working in the studio with John, and Dave White, who had just returned from three years on the road with, CLANG! ... ED SHEERAN. With Dave on engineering duties, it has put us in a good position for when we decide to do another one, but part of me died when Alan did. I haven't written anything since and have no current plans. When that creative urge comes back, Sunshine Corner Studio's will be ready to go.

## CHAPTER 32
## ... FAM

Many of you will know, but, hopefully, thousands of you wont (thinking potential book sales), that my wife Kerry is a singer. Music plays a major part in our lives, whether it be what's playing in the house or on the radio in the car (I am usually outvoted if my daughter Lola is in the car and subjected to Kiss FM). Over the years, Kezza and I have done countless gigs together, some amazing, some not so amazing, and some pretty shocking, usually when alcohol is involved for the latter. We met through a band years ago when she turned up to sing backing vocals. Love at first sight is a reality. Right there and then my life turned on its head. Ten minutes later when she was demonstrating how she could do a handless cartwheel I realised I had met my soul mate. They say behind every great man is a great woman. This is true unless she is the singer and you are the drummer, which has happened numerous times.

When I got asked to play drums with the 'Q The Music Show', I knew our roles were going to be hugely reversed. You see Kez fronts the fabulous James Bond show, which features fifteen musicians, as well as dancers, and even former Bond girls as narrators. It's amazing, and one of my biggest challenges, as it's a readers gig, and a reader I am not. By this I mean that all the musicians are, predominantly, RAF trained classical musicians and so are reading the sheet music. My music teacher gave up with my reading skills back in the early 80's, so I had to learn the show by ear and write it down in my own interpretation. It would be like you being given a page of Bulgarian poems if you read my notes.

Anyway, I put the hours in, and it was time to sit behind my own personal Shirley Bassey. The one thing missing in my world was a tuxedo. I left it late and, on the morning of the show, ran into the high street and perused the charity shops. I was only doing two shows so I wasn't going to shell out for an expensive suit that would sit in my wardrobe. Kez and I have a brilliant system for social events that she knows I wouldn't enjoy. It basically means she takes her gay best friend, Gareth, who is always up for a posh night out and looks amazing in a tux. Couldn't love that man more, for those evenings where they are out schmoozing and I'm at home on the sofa, in my pants, eating crisps, while watching Match of the day, with the dog. Anyway, back to the charity shops, and time was running out, as were my charro options. Sue Ryder was my last hope. The lovely old lady behind the till said she thought she had seen a tux in my size that very morning, but couldn't remember where. She went to that magic little backroom where local good people are ploughing through other people's old clobber, trying to decide what to keep and what to bin, and how much they should overcharge for things. After what seemed like an hour, she finally came back with a tux in her hand which was 'my size'. I was so late; I thanked her profusely and gave her a tenner.

Later that day, after soundchecking 'Diamonds are forever' behind my glamorous wife, there was just an hour to go until showtime. The rest of the musicians pulled out their expensive tuxedo's, from their expensive suit carriers, with their ridiculously shiny shoes. It was at this point I realised I had forgotten the whole 'shoe' scenario and was wearing a pair of black 'Vans', which I would have to try and sneak under the radar. The tried and tested, 'No one will notice as I'm sat behind a drum kit', doesn't work at posh theatre shows, as you have to go to the front at the end and take a bow. The shoes weren't the biggest problem. The jacket fitted like a glove. The trousers on the other hand looked like they had been worn by MC Hammer. So, as I stood surrounded by slick fitted classical musicians looking like James Bond doubles, I awaited the inevitable. Her being in her own dressing room at this point, and texting me saying, 'come and show me your tux'. Part of me hoped that was a typo and that my luck was in, but deep down I knew what she meant. I knocked on the door. She opened, standing in a sensational glittering gold ball gown, looking a million dollars. She smiled, then looked me up and down. There was a pause, she looked me square in the eye, then burst out laughing and, at the top of her voice, began singing, 'Can't touch this, der der der der, der der, der der.' She then took a photo and put it straight on Facebook with the words 'OMG I'm married to MC Hammer'. After that, the gig was easy.

We used to play a duo gig local to where we live, me playing guitar and both of us singing. It was always a funny night, as we invited all our friends and more tellingly, we knew the manager who would give us free drinks. A lot of free drinks. One evening, we decided to make our way through the cocktail menu, with a review of each drink between the songs. This was proving very popular with the crowd, who all decided to join in. By ten o'clock everyone was as sozzled as were we, with a second set still to be performed. That second hour is now in the history books as the 'Married set'. From what I can gather from the people present who were driving, Kez and I spent the hour trying to outdo each other, in order to prove who was the most popular. This was achieved by seeing who could get the most applause after each song. Obviously when it comes to singing, she is in a different league, but I had the power. Basically, I decided the best way to put her in her place was play songs, that were already really high to sing, in a different key to normal. She was pretty spannered on mojito's by this point, and couldn't quite get her head around the fact that the songs sounded different to usual. I thought it was hilarious, but she still won because however high I played the song, her voice is so strong she still managed to hit the high notes. Just. The next day when she woke up, she couldn't speak. When I told her what I had been doing, and after she got her voice back, she didn't speak to me for three days.

Writing this book has been fascinating and quite cathartic. It's brought back memories I hadn't stirred for years. It opened old memories I hadn't thought about for a very long time. Television programmes from when I was younger sprang to mind. Thunderbirds on a Sunday afternoon, classic American cop shows on every evening at nine o'clock, like Starsky and Hutch, Hawaii Five-O, and Charlie's Angels. It still begs the classic question, which angel was your favourite? Or, if you're on a tour bus late at night after a huge amount of alcohol being consumed, the delightful, drunken, musician version, 'what order would you do them in?' Phillistines. In my teens I got heavily into Dallas. I've no idea why, a guilty pleasure, but I watched it for years. Same with Cheers. All these bits of terrestrial TV gold, sitting in the back of my mind, have been stirred by writing this book. I remember when my girls were babies. I always offered to do the night feed. This was because

I had a James Bond film lined up on pause, ready, whilst collecting my brownie points.

So, here we are then, up to speed, and a little more than a quarter of the way through 2020. I am incredibly blessed with the love of a beautiful wife and three happy, and healthy, children, who I'm very proud of. Family means everything to me, and it casts its net far and wide into the realms of parents, brothers, sisters, nieces, and nephews. Add to this, friends who I adore. I turned fifty last year and we rented a big house by the sea and filled it with close pals. It was so touching to have people there I have known for decades, as well as friends who have entered my life in later years. Add to this my beautiful musical families in Alarm and Archive world and I can genuinely say I am the luckiest man alive. To still be here for one, and to be doing what I dreamt of as a child is heaven sent and I am truly grateful.

Everything written in this book is from a happy and positive perspective, with my tongue very firmly in my cheek, and if anyone is in the slightest bit offended, please don't be. There are no digs at anyone in the book, well maybe one. Laugh along to these fabulous stories about fabulous people and let's all enjoy this wonderful life we've been given. There are quite a few references to Mercedes cars and urinals too, I noticed ... Coincidence? I hope so.

Finally, and to end with, here's my favourite all time joke.

A man wakes up in a hospital bed with the doctor standing over him.

The doctor says, 'I've got good news and bad news Sir.'

The man says, 'What's the bad news?'

'Well Sir, I'm afraid your notes got mixed up, and we have amputated your left leg by mistake.'

'Oh my goodness; well, what's the good news?'

'The man in the next bed wants to buy your slippers!'

Peace and love friends ... SMILEY X

## THANKS TO

Everyone in the book. You are there for a reason, a good humoured reason, and because you're all ace.

To all my family and friends. Big Love and Thanks to you all.

To my little book helpers; Trevor Dutton, Simon Elledge, James Walsh, Sue Harley, Chris Russell, Sarah Coppen & Kasey Cassells.

To my fabulous Alarm & Archive families. To Infinity... And Beyond.

Special thanks to Karl Parsons for his Artistic Awesomeness & Jules and Mike for this crazy idea.

And most importantly, my inner sanctum... Kerry, Georgia, Jack & Lola... All you need is Love.

Dedicated to Alan Thompson & Danny Schultz.

WEBSITES

www.smileysfriends.co.uk

www.sunshinecornerstudios.co.uk

www.thealarm.com

www.archiveofficial.uk

www.lovehopestrength.org

www.pearldrum.com

www.zildjian.com

www.vicfirth.com

www.protectionracket.com

www.codedrumheads.co.uk

www.nonutscymbalsleeves.com

www.porteranddavies.co.uk

www.kodishclothing.com

www.gatecrashthepartybooks.com